THOSE COURAGEOUS WOMEN OF THE CIVIL WAR

KAREN ZEINERT

The Millbrook Press
Brookfield, Connecticut

Photographs courtesy of The Granger Collection: cover, p. 59; Brown Brothers: p. 6; The Bettmann Archive: pp. 7, 22, 26, 35, 42, 47, 54, 74, 82; Culver Pictures: p. 15; Archive Photos: pp. 17, 79; Schomburg Center for Research in Black Culture: p. 28; North Wind Picture Archives: p. 39; Stock Montage, Inc.: p. 68; National Portrait Gallery, Smithsonian Institution/Art Resource, NY: p. 71; Harriet Beecher Stowe Center, Hartford, CT: p. 87. Map by Joe LeMonnier

Published by The Millbrook Press, Inc.
2 Old New Milford Road, Brookfield, Connecticut 06804

Library of Congress Cataloging-in-Publication Data
Zeinert, Karen
Those courageous women of the Civil War / Karen Zeinert.
p.   cm.
Includes bibliographical references and index.
Summary: Examines the important contributions of various women, Northern, Southern, and slave, to the American Civil War, on the battlefield, in print, on the home front, and in other areas where they challenged traditional female roles.
ISBN 0-7613-0212-3 (lib. bdg.)
1. United States—History—Civil War, 1861-1865—Women—Juvenile literature. 2. Women—United States—History—19th century—Juvenile literature. [1. United States—History—Civil War, 1861-1865—Women. 2. Women—History—19th century.] I. Title.
E628.Z45   1998   973.7'082—dc21   97-21485   CIP   AC

CONTENTS

CHAPTER ONE

IN A HOUSE DIVIDED

We go to meet our fate in our best bonnets and with smiling faces.

Margaret McLean, upon leaving
Washington, D.C., for the Confederacy

Kady Brownell slept very little during the night of July 20–21, 1861. Instead, she stared into the darkness and waited for the signal that would call her to action. At 2 A.M. she finally heard the drums. She dressed quickly, grabbed her flag, and fell in line with the soldiers of the 1st Rhode Island Infantry. Within the hour they began their march to Bull Run, an important railhead 20 miles (32 kilometers) southwest of Washington, D.C. Kady was on her way to the first major battle of the Civil War.

While Kady was marching, many men and women around Washington packed picnic lunches and piled into carriages. They, too, were going to Bull Run—not to fight but to watch what was predicted to be a glorious battle. One spectator was so confident that the North would beat the South and then push on to capture the South's capital in Richmond that afternoon that he brought along his dancing shoes for a victory ball in the defeated city that night.

Kady Brownell

The first major battle of the Civil War occurred at Bull Run, Virginia, where the Union Army was overpowered by the Confederates. Kady Brownell was a color bearer with the 1st Rhode Island Infantry and retreated when the enemy was just a few hundred yards away.

Kady marched with Brigadier General Irvin McDowell. He moved southward with more than 30,000 men to square off with a 23,000-man Southern force under the command of Brigadier General P.G.T. Beauregard. Kady's job was that of color bearer. Until now, she had only carried her infantry's flag in parades and drills. Today Kady would mark a spot on the battlefield with her flag where her infantry was to rally should its plans go awry.

Although Northerners anticipated victory, General Beauregard's men seized the upper hand. When they boldly charged the Northern regiments, Brigadier General McDowell's men panicked. Kady saw her infantry in retreat, and she waved her flag high in the air, shouting to the soldiers to rally. But the men of the 1st Infantry—as well as quite a few other Northerners—just wanted to get off the battlefield. Kady remained in her position until the enemy was only a few hundred yards away before she, too, retreated.

Northern troops and spectators raced pell-mell back to Washington. The man with the dancing shoes was in such a hurry to leave that he dropped his lunch and shoes. He at least reached safety. More than 1,000 Northerners, both soldiers and spectators, were captured, including two congressmen.

Few Americans were surprised that the North and South were embroiled in a civil war. The two sections had been arguing for years over issues for which there seemed to be no solution.

The North, which was home to 92 percent of the nation's industries in 1861, favored a strong centralized government. It wanted Congress to build railroads to help manufacturers and Midwest farmers get their products to market more easily. And it also wanted the federal government to place high tariffs, or taxes, on manufactured goods coming into the country so that Americans would be less eager to buy foreign-made products and more inclined to purchase locally made ones.

On the other hand, Southerners wanted as many decisions as possible left to the states. And the South, which had a fine network of rivers on which to transport its products to market—primarily cotton, tobacco, and rice—was not eager to pay for railroads in the North. Also, the South, which sold tons of cotton overseas, wanted lower taxes on products it imported from its European trading partners.

But of all the issues that divided America, it was the practice of slavery that drew the most attention and caused the most emotional debates. Many Northerners wanted Congress to forbid slavery in the new territories that were being added as the country expanded westward in the 1800s. Some of these Northerners, called abolitionists, wanted to go even further; they wanted to outlaw slavery altogether.

Southerners refused to put limits on slavery, let alone end it. They pointed out that the South, which had a serious shortage of workers, needed slaves to plant, tend, and harvest its crops. In addition, slave owners insisted that slavery not only was essential to the success of the Southern economy, but slaves were a major investment. How, owners wondered, could they be expected to simply free 3.5 million workers, some of whom were valued at more than $1,000 each? Besides, said the owners, who gave Northerners the right to tell Southerners what to do?

The issue of slavery was also tied to a struggle for power in Congress. Southern congressmen wanted more slave states because the representatives from such states would most likely vote with them. These votes would enable Southerners to control Congress and pass laws that would help the South. But Northern congressmen were equally determined to control the legislature, so they fought every Southern effort to increase the number of slave states.

Therefore, whenever a territory applied for statehood, one of the major issues to be decided was whether it was to enter the Union as a free state or a slave state. Over the years, the struggle for power intensified; tempers flared, and debates between Northern and Southern congressmen turned into shouting matches.

Even though it was extremely difficult to do so, Congress managed to work out compromises in 1820 and 1850 to ease tensions between the two sections. The 1820 agreement, the Missouri Compromise, maintained a balance of free and slave states. In addition, Congress divided the remaining territory then held by the United States along the 36° 30' parallel. In the future, any part of this territory located south of the parallel that applied for statehood could enter the Union as a slave state; any territory north of the line would enter the Union as a free state.

In the late 1840s the United States obtained land from Mexico, and an agreement governing these new territories was necessary. The result was the Compromise of 1850. This agreement allowed people in the territories (other than California, which would enter as a free state, and Texas, which had already entered the Union as a slave state) to decide for themselves if they would permit slavery. The compromise also called for a stricter enforcement of the Fugitive Slave Law to help Southerners reclaim their runaway slaves. Since it was unlikely that the United States would be adding any large territory in the near future, Congress hoped that its debate over slavery had ended.

But the slave issue just wouldn't go away. In 1854 the Kansas-Nebraska Act was passed despite howls and objections put forth by some outraged Northerners. This act gave the Kansas and Nebraska territories, both of which had been declared free in 1820 because they were north of the 36° 30' line, the right to have slaves if the citizens there voted to do so. Proslavery and anti-slavery supporters clashed in Kansas, and before federal troops could restore order, more than 200 people had been killed. Stunned by the bloodshed in Kansas, most Americans once again tried to find a peaceful solution to the slavery issue.

Meanwhile a few abolitionists, believing that violence was the only way to end slavery, began to arm themselves for battle. One of these abolitionists was John Brown, who had led deadly attacks against supporters of slavery in Kansas. In October 1859, Brown and eighteen of his followers marched on Harpers Ferry, Virginia. Here Brown hoped to seize guns and ammunition worth several million dollars that could be used to arm slaves for an all-out rebellion. Brown managed to take the arsenal as planned, but he and his followers were captured at Harpers Ferry shortly afterward. Brown was arrested, tried, convicted of treason, and hanged.

As soon as Southerners heard about Brown's raid, they became frightened. They were convinced that the entire North was planning to invade the South and free the slaves by force. Elizabeth Van Lew, who lived in Richmond, Virginia, noted that from the time of Brown's raid, "Our people were in a palpable state of war. The alarm bells would be rung, the tramp of armed men [who gathered to defend the city] heard through the night."[1]

Southerners were even more frightened when Abraham Lincoln was elected president in 1860. They believed that Lincoln was an abolitionist. Hadn't he said, they asked, that a house divided against itself, half slave, half free, couldn't stand? Didn't this mean that he meant to free the slaves? Lincoln was so feared in the South that he didn't receive a single vote in ten of the thirteen slave states.

By late 1860, Southern leaders saw no future for their states in the Union. They believed that the spread of slavery into new territories was doomed, and that this would eventually result in the North's control of the legislature. Congress could then outlaw slavery altogether, which would destroy the South's economy, as well as pass other unfavorable legislation. To retain control over their affairs, Southern leaders called on all slave states to secede and form a new country.

Shortly after Southern leaders called for secession, representatives in Alabama, Florida, Georgia, Louisiana, Mississippi, South Carolina, and Texas held meetings in their state capitals. Each of the delegations, sometimes after a month or more of debate, voted to secede. In February 1861, representatives from these states met in Montgomery, Alabama, to form the Confederate States of America. This new country then asked the other slave states—Arkansas, Delaware, Kentucky, Maryland, Missouri, North Carolina, Tennessee, and Virginia—to join it. All but Delaware, Maryland, Missouri, and Kentucky ultimately agreed to do so.

While Southerners voted on the issue of secession, Northerners looked on with disbelief. They insisted that no state could leave the Union for any reason at any time. Secession, they argued, was a blow to the basic democratic idea that the majority should rule. If Southern states could leave when they didn't get their way, what, Northerners asked, would prevent others from doing the same thing, destroying the Union in the process? Angry Northerners shook their fists and called Confederates "fools" and "treasonous villains" and vowed to go to war to keep the country together.

When the war began, both sides believed that the conflict would be short. But the North underestimated the South's determination to fight for its independence, and Southerners misjudged the North's will to preserve the United States. The short war everyone had anticipated—sixty days long at the most—became a four-year ordeal of hard-fought, bloody battles.

By 1865, more than 600,000 men had died in the conflict. This tragic loss is nearly equal to the number of American casualties in all of America's other wars combined—the Revolutionary War (1775–1783), the War of 1812 (1812–1815), the Mexican War (1846–1848), the Spanish-American War (1898), World War I (1917–1918), World War II (1941–1945), the Korean War (1950–1953), the Vietnam War (1964–1975), and the Persian Gulf War (1991).

Once both sides realized that the conflict would be anything but short, they began to mobilize all their available resources. Factories produced munitions and uniforms as fast as possible. Southern farmers stopped raising cotton and started

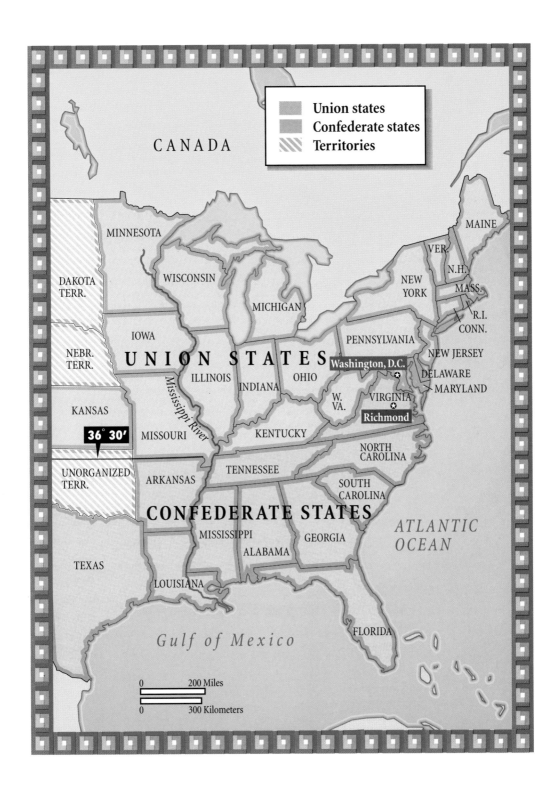

Union states
Confederate states
Territories

CANADA

MINNESOTA

DAKOTA
TERR.

WISCONSIN

MICHIGAN

IOWA

NEBR.
TERR.

UNION STATES

ILLINOIS   INDIANA   OHIO

KANSAS

36° 30'

MISSOURI

KENTUCKY

ARKANSAS

TENNESSEE

UNORGANIZED
TERR.

CONFEDERATE STATES

MISSISSIPPI

ALABAMA   GEORGIA

TEXAS

LOUISIANA

Mississippi River

MAINE

VER.

N.H.

NEW
YORK

MASS.

R.I.
CONN.

PENNSYLVANIA

NEW JERSEY

Washington, D.C.

DELAWARE

MARYLAND

W.
VA.

VIRGINIA

Richmond

NORTH
CAROLINA

SOUTH
CAROLINA

ATLANTIC
OCEAN

FLORIDA

Gulf of Mexico

0   200 Miles

0   300 Kilometers

to grow crops that soldiers could eat. When fewer and fewer men volunteered to fight, the Confederacy, then the Union, passed laws that enabled the government to draft soldiers—in effect, ordering men to fight.

Before the crisis began, women were considered too frail and emotional to become involved in wartime activities. In the 1860s, according to one gentleman of the day, the ideal woman was "nervous, fickle, capricious, delicate, diffident and dependent."[2] These characteristics were considered attractive and even thought to be worthy of worship. Popular women's magazines gave tips on how to become such a woman.

Clothing styles, especially among the wealthy, emphasized women's supposed frailty. Tiny waists, 20 inches (50 centimeters) or less, were the rage, and in order to achieve this ideal, women wore corsets that were laced as tightly as possible. This made breathing difficult, and it was not uncommon for ladies to be light-headed or even to faint on occasion. Also, it was not uncommon for women to need assistance moving about when they wore long, excessively full skirts over hoops too wide to pass through a narrow doorway.

Not all women—4 million in the South, including slaves, and 9 million in the North—were dependent ladies dressed in cumbersome clothing. Although their lives varied greatly from one section of the country to another in 1860, women were much stronger and less dependent than some men and magazine editors would admit.

In the New England states, industry was booming. As a result, many families had more income than ever before. They bought large homes and filled them with heavy carpets, big stoves with brass trim, velvet drapes, and lots of furniture. Wives, in addition to feeding and clothing their families, were expected to maintain these belongings. So they hung their hoops on pegs, dragged carpets and drapes outside to air, and polished tables and brass until they were bright and shiny.

Despite their time-consuming duties, these women, some of whom had received fine educations, wanted more from life than unending household duties. Many wanted to work for causes in which they believed. Some became swept up in the slavery issue, and they joined the abolitionists. Others supported the suffrage movement, which was fighting for the right for women to vote. A daring few even argued for dress reform. They ridiculed corsets and hoops and advocated trousers for the modern woman. In the process of fighting for change, these women learned how to organize and how to make an association successful.

Women's fashions of the 1860s, with their cinched waists and wide hoop skirts, made it difficult for women to move around freely and tended to make them docile and dependent. While this behavior was fashionable at the time, most women could not afford to dress this way.

Less fortunate women did not have time to participate in such associations. Caring for children and trying to provide for their families took most of their energy. Because these women lacked the money to buy manufactured products, they had to make their own clothing, soap, and candles (if they could not afford oil lanterns) all of which were time-consuming activities.

In rural areas of the North and South, women also worked hard. They maintained homes, helped with farm chores, chopped wood, carried water, and tended vegetable and herb gardens. The herbs were used for medicinal purposes. In the country, doctors were few and far between, and when illness struck, wives and mothers were expected to know what to do. Because many of these families did not have large incomes, family members had to learn to make the most of every possession. Women routinely "turned out" worn, faded clothing, recycling them by taking garments apart and sewing them back together with the wrong side on the outside, adding new cuffs and collars.

Although jobs were scarce outside the home for women in the country, some managed to make a living as a midwife (one who delivers babies) or as a teacher. Both of these occupations were socially acceptable because they were an extension of a woman's traditional household duties, which included nursing and bringing up children. Because salaries for teachers were low, teachers often were offered room and board with their pupils' families, moving from one home to another throughout the school year.

Women who lived on plantations in the South, contrary to popular stories about that time, did not have a life of leisure. Because plantations were far from cities, most estates were as self-sufficient as possible. The mistress supervised the vegetable garden, the manufacture of clothes, and the ordering of supplies. She also supervised the slaves' quarters, tended the sick, and trained the house slaves. In many cases, mistresses worked with their slaves. Sarah Espy, who managed a plantation in Alabama, once helped her slaves butcher fifteen hogs in a single day.

Southern women were not as outspoken or as involved in public affairs as Northern women were. This was because, in part, the South often was more tradition-bound than the North. In addition, women who spoke out were thought to be in league with the abolitionists and the suffragists and were regarded with contempt.

Among the hardest workers of all, North and South, were female slaves. These women worked twelve to sixteen hours per day six days a week. Generally, slaves were divided into two groups, household servants and field hands. Servants, who cooked, cleaned, and did the laundry, were sometimes taught

Before the Civil War, female slaves, whether they were household servants or field hands, had no control over their lives and no hope to gain freedom. Here a woman and a girl do the washing while a younger girl minds a baby.

special skills such as dyeing fabrics or making medications. Field hands plowed the land, plucked worms from tobacco leaves, split rails, and made bricks. One former slave recalled that she had "done ever thing on a farm what a man done 'cept cut wheat."[3]

Slave women had no control over their lives. They were expected to work hard without complaint and bear children who might be sold to an owner on another plantation. As young women, they lived in fear of possible sexual assault by their owners or overseers. As old women, when they could no longer work hard, some faced the humiliation of having their owner pay another to take them off his hands.

Although many dreamed of freedom, most lacked the means to make this dream come true. Escape was sometimes possible, but slaves had to have something to escape to, a place to live and some way to support themselves. Besides, there was always a chance that a runaway would be caught, and the severe beating that would follow was enough to make any slave think twice about becoming a fugitive. The Underground Railroad helped many slaves reach safety and start new lives, but it could not free all of them.

Until the Civil War began, few slaves had any hope of gaining their freedom. But once the conflict started, some slaves close to Union lines managed to slip away at night and find safety with the soldiers. Irate slave owners demanded that their property be returned. They were not successful. Instead, soldiers and former slaves built temporary shelters near forts to house runaways, whose numbers grew throughout the war. At one point, more than 900 blacks were housed near Fort Monroe in Virginia.

In 1863, President Lincoln issued the Emancipation Proclamation. This proclaimed that slaves would be free in any territory that the Union conquered in the Confederacy. Needless to say, those who were still enslaved hoped and prayed that the

North would take their state soon, and it is no wonder that slaves fell to their knees and gave prayers of thanksgiving at the first sight of Union troops.

Even though the ideal woman, other than a slave, was supposed to be delicate, necessity forced Northern and Southern women to play a significant role in the war. Some, like Kady Brownell, served on the battlefield. Others spied for their side, nursed the wounded, made uniforms and munitions, and managed the home front. These women displayed gritty determination and made incredible sacrifices while helping the cause in which they so deeply believed. The history of the Civil War would not be complete without their stories.

CHAPTER TWO

ON THE BATTLEFIELD

I . . . saw the enemy before me and was inspired by an eager desire to conquer him . . . so, when by the general's command, we were [ordered] to fall back, I was overcome with rage.

Loreta Janeta Velazquez,
Confederate officer

From the beginning of the Civil War, women served on the battlefield. In fact, in addition to Kady Brownell, at least two other women, Marie Tebe and Loreta Velazquez, were in the line of fire at the first Battle of Bull Run.

Marie Tebe, who held the record for serving the longest as a color bearer, remained on duty for three years. She first enlisted in the Union's 27th Pennsylvania Volunteers with her husband on April 16, 1861. Tebe, who drew a regular soldier's pay of $12 per month, was under fire in at least thirteen battles. Her bravery impressed the commander of the 114th Pennsylvania Volunteers, and he persuaded her to join his troops. She marched with the 114th until late 1864. Although Marie faced danger often, she was wounded only once.

In the beginning of the war, many units, North and South, had female flag bearers, or *vivandières*, like Brownell and Tebe. Most of the women were chaperoned by a male relative, usually a husband or brother, to protect their reputations, and the majority were little more than colorful ornaments for the army—pretty ladies dressed in eye-catching uniforms. Mary Chesnut was so taken by the sighting of her first *vivandière* in Richmond that she included a description of the young woman in her journal: "She was dressed in the uniform of her regiment, but wore Turkish pantaloons. She frisked about in her hat and feathers . . . played the piano; and sang war songs. . . . She was followed at every step by a mob of admiring soldiers and boys."[1]

It was one thing to march in a parade with the soldiers; it was quite a different experience to be on the battlefield with them. Once everyone realized that the war was to be anything but short and glorious and that the enemy shot at color-bearers, many units refused to let women hold flags during a battle. Although many *vivandières* were sent home, a few remained to carry the flag during drills and to take on new responsibilities. They nursed the wounded when no one else was available, and they tried to comfort those men who were beyond medical attention. More than one soldier later recalled seeing a *vivandière* cradling the head of a dying soldier in her arms.

Since only men could enlist as soldiers then, Loreta Velazquez, a Confederate officer, had to disguise herself in order to serve. If her true identity had been discovered, she would have faced ridicule from her peers as well as from the public.

Velazquez had been intrigued by war all her life. She loved to read, and even as a child her favorite subjects were soldiers and battles. She was especially taken by stories about Joan of Arc, a young Frenchwoman who led soldiers into battle against an English army in France in 1429. Loreta wrote in her memoirs: "I longed for an opportunity to become another such as she."[2] It's not surprising, then, that Velazquez, eager for adventure and devoted to the Confederacy, became caught up in the war effort.

What is surprising is the ease with which she was able to join the Confederate forces. One reason is that recruiting agents did not believe that ladies would even think about taking to the battlefield, let alone actually doing it. Another is that physical examinations for enlistment were not very thorough. In any case, shortly after the war began, Velazquez left her home in New Orleans and purchased a commission (officer's title), which was a common practice in the 1800s.

Loreta Velazquez served under her husband in the Confederate Army, disguised as a man known as Harry T. Buford. She was one of an estimated four hundred women who fought in the war disguised as men.

From then on, she was known as Lieutenant Harry T. Buford. She eventually attached herself to a regiment from Alabama, where she served with General Barnard Bee.

On July 21, 1861, while spectators were racing toward Bull Run, Loreta was preparing for her first battle. Later she wrote:

> The supreme moment of my life had arrived, and all the glorious aspirations of my romantic girlhood were on the point of realization. I was elated beyond measure, although coolheaded enough. . . . Fear was a word I did not know the meaning of; and as I noted the ashy faces and the trembling limbs of some of the men about me, I almost wished that I could feel a little fear, if only for the sake of sympathizing with the poor devils.[3]

As the two sides struggled for victory, Loreta enjoyed the excitement of the battle so much that when her superior ordered a withdrawal, she flew into a rage. She calmed down a bit when she realized that he was simply retreating to regroup for another charge.

Velazquez fought other battles in the area in the defense of Richmond. At one point, she led her company when her superiors had been killed or taken prisoner. In time, though,

Loreta, like many soldiers, tired of battle. She then volunteered to work for the Confederacy as a spy, and she was sent North to determine the enemy's strength.

Brownell, Tebe, and Velazquez may have been the only women serving at Bull Run, but they were hardly the only women on the battlefield during the war. Historians believe that at least 400 women served as soldiers, in disguise, from 1861 to 1865. Some helped the North achieve three important goals: capturing Richmond, taking control of the Mississippi River to divide and weaken the South, and erecting a naval blockade around the Confederacy's coast to prevent the Southern states from receiving supplies. Those fighting for the South helped fortify its borders to prevent an invasion and waited for the enemy to come.

Many of the women's identities will never be known; some were never unmasked, and of those who were, many refused to give their true names. One young woman who joined the 14th Iowa Infantry feared public humiliation when she was discovered. She became so upset that she committed suicide.

To avoid detection, most women moved about often. This was easy enough to do, since many enlistments were for a period of only ninety days. Lizzie Compton, who first served with the Union's Army of the Potomac when she was fourteen years old, was unable to successfully disguise the fact that she was a female. Her real sex was discovered at least seven times. When she was told to leave and never show her face in the army again, she simply looked about for another unit that would take her.

Unlike Compton, Jennie Hodgers had little difficulty disguising herself. She served as a Union soldier for three years, and her real identity was not discovered until forty-five years after the war ended.

Jennie, who called herself Albert Cashier, enlisted in Illinois on August 6, 1862. Her regiment, along with many others from the Midwest, was assigned to the Mississippi River campaign. Fifteen boats full of soldiers, mules, horses, and wagons began a week-long trip down the Mississippi on January 19, 1863. They stopped short of Vicksburg, the South's last stronghold on the river.

Vicksburg was well fortified by Confederate soldiers. At first, Union General Ulysses S. Grant, who was in charge of taking control of the Mississippi, tried to take the city by force. His soldiers advanced in large numbers, but when they suffered serious losses, he decided to lay siege to the city. He cut off all incoming sources of food and repeatedly shelled the city to destroy morale. This was effective, but it took almost two months for the Union to accomplish its goal.

The fall of Vicksburg meant that the Union now controlled the entire Mississippi River. This cut the Confederacy into two parts and made it impossible for the South to move supplies on or across the river.

After the fall of Vicksburg, Jennie Hodgers participated in battles in northern Mississippi, Tennessee, and Alabama. When she left the army, she had taken part in forty battles and skirmishes without being wounded or discovered.

After the war, she returned to Illinois. She settled down in Saunemin, where she continued to disguise herself. It wasn't until she was injured in an accident in 1911 and needed medical care that her true sex was discovered. Because she had been a soldier, she was eligible for treatment in a veterans hospital. With the blessing of the hospital's administration, Hodgers was admitted—in disguise—as Albert Cashier.

Strangely enough, while almost all female soldiers hid their true identify, at least one female soldier enlisted as a woman and was accepted. Maria Lewis joined the 8th New York Cavalry when it reached Alexandria, Virginia. Lewis, a former slave, fled to the Union lines as soon as she thought that she could reach the soldiers without getting caught by her owner. She not only fought like the rest of the soldiers, but she traveled with the men to Washington to present twenty-two Confederate banners that the regiment had seized to the War Department. Why she was accepted is not clear. However, unlike the soldiers in her unit, she was familiar with the area, and her expertise as a potential scout may have outweighed the fact that she was a woman.

The most controversial women associated with the army were the camp followers. These women, usually wives of the soldiers, traveled with the army. They earned their keep and the keep of their children by cooking meals for the troops and washing their clothes. Many followers also served as unofficial nurses. However, some of the camp followers were prostitutes, and as rumors about their presence spread, all women in camp became suspect.

Women did not have to be on the battlefield to help their army. At the beginning of the war, they were active in encouraging their husbands, boyfriends, and sons of fighting age—4 million in the North, 1 million in the South—to join the army. Sarah Emma Edmonds, a Union nurse and spy, who disguised herself as a man throughout most of the war, said that Southern women were "the best recruiting officers," avoiding "any young man who refuses to enlist."[4] But as the war dragged on and shocking losses on the battlefield were recorded—23,000 casualties alone in the battle at Shiloh, Tennessee—many women refused to put such pressure on young men.

Women also helped the army by preparing to serve as volunteers to defend the home front should the enemy break through their soldiers' lines. A women's drill team was started in New York in 1861. In the South, many girls' schools included lessons in shooting, and more than one young lady vowed "to kill the first Yankee who came within sight of their homes."[5] Sallie Reneau of Mississippi offered to raise a company of women to be armed, uniformed, and paid like soldiers to defend the home front, but her offer was turned down.

Women, often the wives of soldiers, washed laundry and cooked for the troops. With their children in tow, they lived as families while the armies were camped semi-permanently.

In Bascom, Georgia, a home guard was formed entirely of women. One of the members described her group in a letter to a friend:

> We have formed a Female Company in Bascom for the purpose of learning to shoot, so that if all the men go to war [we] can protect our homes and selves. . . . The name of our company is the Bascom Home Guards. You know how nervous the timid Mollie was. Well, now she can load and fire and hit a spot at a good distance. . . . We are all delighted with the idea of learning to shoot. Father says he thinks our uniform is prettier than the boys although ours is made of common calico."[6]

In LaGrange, Georgia, a group known as the Nancy Harts, in honor of the Revolutionary War heroine, organized a local militia to defend the city and keep law and order. The Harts had forty members, who paraded and drilled in town after target practice for the purpose of "inspiring their friends with confidence and striking terror to the hearts of would-be evil doers. . . . Their reputation as markswomen became widespread."[7]

Even though many armed women would never fire a shot at the enemy during the war, their lives had been greatly affected by the war, for few before the conflict would have considered joining a regiment or a local militia. And these women were not the only ones to drastically alter their attitudes and their lives.

SUSIE KING TAYLOR

Susie King Taylor gained her freedom from slavery in 1862 when Union soldiers drove Confederate forces out of Fort Pulaski, near Savannah, Georgia. Fleeing Confederates left their slaves behind. Union forces then recruited a regiment of former male slaves. Taylor, who was married to one of the regiment's soldiers, became a camp follower. At first she was a laundress. Later she helped care for weapons as well:

> I learned to handle a musket very well while in the regiment, and could shoot straight and often hit the target. I assisted in cleaning the guns and used to fire them off, to see if the cartridges were dry, before cleaning and reloading, each day. I thought this great fun. I was also able to take a gun all apart, and put it together again.[8]

In the evening, she taught fellow blacks how to read and write. Susie was among the few slaves who had been educated by their owners even though Southern laws outlawed such an education. After the war, she ran a school for former slaves.

CHAPTER THREE

SPYING FOR THE CAUSE

I was highly commended by the commanding general for my coolness [during my escape from Confederate pickets] but was told kindly and candidly that I would not be permitted to go out again in that vicinity in the capacity of a spy, as I would most assuredly meet with some of those who had seen me . . . and I would consequently be hung up to the nearest tree.

Sarah Emma Edmonds,
Union spy

At the beginning of the Civil War, both sides had many women who offered to spy for their cause even though this meant risking their lives. These spies included women who were willing to go behind enemy lines as well as those who suddenly found themselves in enemy territory when the United States was torn asunder—for example, Union supporters who lived in Richmond, Virginia, or Southern sympathizers who lived in Washington. Some spies worked throughout the war; others were caught quickly or lost their nerve.

Most spies gave their information to a trusted courier who would then carry it through the enemy's lines. Couriers hid messages in their upswept hairdos, in the hems of their petti-coats, and behind pictures in their lockets. Incredible as it may seem, during the first weeks of the war, some spies actually sent messages through the mail.

One of the most daring and successful Union spies was Elizabeth Van Lew of Richmond. Van Lew was the daughter of a wealthy merchant who left a sizable estate when he died, including a number of slaves. Unlike her father, Elizabeth was an abolitionist at heart, and she immediately freed these slaves, several of whom remained with her as servants. When Virginia seceded, Van Lew announced her support for the Union. She thought that secessionists were traitors, and she said so—often and loudly.

Richmonders had always considered Elizabeth a bit too outspoken for her own good. But because she came from one of the most influential families in the city, townspeople had managed to overlook her views, even her abolitionist stance, which they blamed on her schooling in Philadelphia. However, when Elizabeth refused to support the Confederacy, she had, in their opinion, gone too far. From then on, most people in the city ignored her. This suited her just fine, for she was then able to go about her business without much notice.

Van Lew gathered information in a variety of ways. Fearing for the health of Union soldiers held prisoner in Richmond, she volunteered to take food and medicine to the captives. While she fed the soldiers, she asked lots of questions about what they had seen on their way to prison and what they had heard from their captors and guards.

Van Lew also received information from the Confederate White House. When the capital was set up in Richmond, Elizabeth, whose father had been a friend of Confederate President Jefferson Davis, offered to provide Davis with an able servant, Mary Elizabeth Bowser. Bowser, one of Van Lew's former slaves whom she had sent to Philadelphia to be educated, was devoted to her mistress and deeply opposed to the Confederacy. When Davis accepted Van Lew's offer, Bowser gladly returned to Richmond seeing this assignment as an opportunity to spy for the Union.

To get messages out of Richmond, which was surrounded by guards, Van Lew devised several schemes. One of her most common methods required the help of one of her servants and a former slave, Elizabeth Draper Mitchell. Van Lew owned a small farm just outside the city, and for years Mitchell had been going to this farm on a daily basis to collect eggs and fresh produce. Continuing this practice would not raise suspicion, so Van Lew made the most of it. Mitchell, in addition to carrying empty baskets to the farm, carried messages in a hollowed-out section in the heel of her shoe. The messages were then picked up at the farm and carried to another relay station, one of five established for passing on information.

On occasion, Van Lew delivered messages herself. Disguised as a simple farmhand, she rode out of town on a horse that she hid in the library of her mansion to prevent Confederate soldiers from taking it for the army.

No matter how the information was delivered, it was well received by the Union. General Ulysses S. Grant, who was the recipient of most of Van Lew's messages at the end of the war when Grant led his drive to defeat Richmond, considered Van Lew one of his most important sources.

Another Union spy, Sarah Emma Edmonds was a master of disguises. Sarah, a Canadian, joined the Union cause by enlisting in the army as Frank Thompson. She served on the battlefield and in field hospitals before agreeing to spy for the Union.

Edmonds was asked to go through Confederate lines in Northern Virginia several times. On one occasion, she cut her hair extra short and disguised herself as a male slave before slipping through picket lines. Shortly after, she joined a group of blacks who were digging trenches for the army near Williamsburg, where she counted guns and soldiers.

Months later she was again asked to go into Confederate territory. This time, she disguised herself as a female peddler. Sarah planned to follow the Confederate Army, selling cakes and pies to the soldiers while gathering information. She abandoned her plan when she fell into a stream and lost her baked goods. Unwilling to give up, Edmonds boldly approached Southern pickets in her bedraggled clothes, telling them that she was a war refugee who wanted nothing more than to find her friends in the South. Sarah's appearance and tears, which she could muster at will, were convincing, and the pickets let her through.

While she was organizing a plan, Sarah took shelter in an abandoned farmhouse. Here she stumbled upon a Confederate officer, Captain Allen Hall, who was seriously ill with typhoid fever. Hall had been too weak to continue to travel with his regiment and, at his request, had been left behind. Edmonds quickly realized that Hall was dying. She made him as comfortable as possible and prepared some food for him. Before Hall passed away, he gave Edmonds his gold watch and a message to be delivered to his headquarters.

The next morning, Sarah was on her way. The captain's watch was as good as a pass, and soon she was talking to officers and absorbing as much information as she could. After borrowing a horse from headquarters, she led several men to Hall's body so that he might have a proper burial. When an opportunity to escape presented itself, Edmonds took off—on the borrowed horse—and although she had several encounters with Confederate pickets, she managed to reach the Union lines.

After a third spying assignment, during which pickets caught her and attempted, unsuccessfully, to hold her, Edmonds returned to being a nurse, again in disguise as Frank Thompson. While she was helping wounded soldiers after the battle at Antietam, one young man in particular caught her eye. This soldier was watching Sarah closely, clearly trying to make a decision. Finally the young man motioned to Edmonds to come closer. After studying Sarah's face for some time, the soldier began to speak:

> I can trust you, and will tell you a secret. I am not what I seem, but am a female. I enlisted from the purest motives, and have remained undiscovered and unsuspected. I have neither father, mother, nor sister. My only brother was killed today. I closed his eyes about an hour before I was wounded. I shall soon be with him. . . . I wish you to bury me with your own hands, that none may know after my death that I am other than my appearance indicates.[1]

Sarah gave her word that she would do so, and she personally buried the young woman. Historians have long wondered if the soldier's selection of Edmonds was a random choice or if she was one of the few to see through Sarah's disguise.

The Union had many other spies, some of whom became well known. These spies included Pauline Cushman, a native of Louisiana, who traveled throughout the South as an actress, gathering information as she went along. Cushman was eventually caught and sentenced to hang. She managed to escape, though, and went on to entertain large audiences in the North with tales about her spying days. Mary Caroline Allan, who lived in Richmond, sent information to Union headquarters. She worked independently. Rebecca Wright, a young schoolteacher in Virginia who supplied General Philip Sheridan with information, also worked independently. And Alvira Smith in Missouri and Anna Campbell in Alabama risked their lives as couriers.

While Northern spies were gathering as much information as they could, spies for the South were also busy at work. They, too, risked their lives, and at least one died while helping her country.

Perhaps the best-known Confederate woman spy was Rose O'Neal Greenhow. Rose, a Marylander by birth, had married Robert Greenhow, a wealthy Washingtonian. She loved company and was a popular hostess. After her husband died, Rose continued to entertain on a grand scale, and at the start of the war, she had many influential friends, including William H. Seward, President Lincoln's secretary of state.

Although Rose's sympathies were clearly on the side of the South, she decided not to leave the Union, unlike many other Southerners and their supporters. Thomas Jordon, a former captain in the U.S. Army who would accept a post in the Confederate Army, asked Rose to use her position in the Union's capital to spy for the South. Greenhow agreed to do so.

Rose's espionage helped the South win the first major battle of the war, at Bull Run. She sifted through all the rumors running rampant in the city, talked to men in the know, and then sent two messages to the Confederacy. The first was carried through Union lines outside Washington by Bettie Duvall; the second was carried through the lines by a former federal employee. Together, the messages gave Confederate leaders an overview of what the Union planned, the number of men that would be involved, and when they would arrive. This enabled the Southern army to be well prepared for the battle.

Greenhow's activities did not go unnoticed. As was true in the aftermath of almost all battles during the war, the losing side suspected that it had been outdone on the battlefield not by a superior fighting force but by a better informed army that had been educated by spies. One month after the battle at Bull Run, Rose's home was searched. When compromising information was found, she and her eight-year-old daughter were placed under house arrest.

Because it was rumored that many dangerous spies were now at work in Washington, secret police agents began to round up suspects. Not wanting to put the delicate ladies among them

Even while under house arrest, Rose Greenhow managed to continue her spying activities for the Confederacy. When she was discovered, she was sent to the Old Capitol prison in Washington, where this picture was taken. With her is her young daughter.

into a prison cell if they could avoid it, the police decided to house the suspects in Greenhow's home, a decision that enraged her. Inmates at "Fort Greenhow," as it became known, included at least ten women. One was an elderly mother of a Confederate officer. Another was despised by Rose, who bristled at the thought of having to share her home with a woman who supposedly had no taste, few social skills, and low moral standards to boot.

Even though it seemed impossible to do, Rose somehow managed to pick up information from her captors and send messages to the Confederacy. Embarrassed secret agents then decided to put her in a secure prison, while it made plans to move her to the Confederacy, where, it was assumed, Greenhow could do the Union no harm. She was placed in the Old Capitol prison in Washington.

On May 31, 1862, Greenhow was taken to Baltimore, and on June 4, she arrived in Richmond, where she was regarded as a heroine. She recorded her arrival in her journal:

> I arrived in Richmond, on the morning of the 4th, and was taken to the best hotel in the place . . . where rooms had been prepared for me. General Winder, the Commandant of Richmond, came immediately to call upon me. . . .
>
> On the evening after my arrival our President did me the honour of calling upon me, and his words of greeting, "But for you there would have been no battle of Bull Run," repaid me for all that I had endured. . . . And I shall ever remember that as the proudest moment of my whole life.[2]

Greenhow continued to work for the Confederacy, even though her spying days were finished. In the summer of 1863, she headed for Europe aboard a blockade runner, a ship designed to outrun and outmaneuver Union patrol ships watching the Confederate coast. Here she delivered letters from President Jefferson Davis to French and British dignitaries. The

Confederacy believed that France and especially Britain, which had been one of the South's major trading partners, could be persuaded to support the South in its struggle for independence. Therefore every contact with the leaders of the two countries was important. Rose not only was well received, but was able to raise significant sums of money to help the South.

When Greenhow returned to the Confederacy in the fall of 1864, again aboard a blockade runner, her ship was spotted by a Union patrol boat as it neared the shore. Fearing arrest, she asked the runner's captain to provide rowers and a small boat to take her ashore. He agreed to do so, but before the boat reached land, it capsized, and Rose was drowned. Legend has it that she was carrying gold meant for the Confederacy, and this weighed her down and made death inescapable.

Although Rose Greenhow may be the best-known Confederate woman spy, the most colorful female agent for the Confederacy was Belle Boyd. Boyd was born in what is now Martinsburg, West Virginia. She was headstrong, beautiful, daring, and only seventeen years old when the war began.

After Union troops occupied Belle's hometown early in the war, the Boyd home became a source of deep concern for federal troops. When stories surfaced about Belle covering the walls of her bedroom with Confederate flags, several soldiers, after having too much to drink, decided to investigate. They staggered to the Boyd home and demanded entry. Belle steadfastly refused to let the men into her home, and she and her mother personally blocked the doorway. The soldiers responded by swearing at the women and threatening them. Belle finally became so angry that she got a revolver and killed one of the soldiers. An army officer was then called to the scene, and after determining that the soldiers were clearly out of line, he placed a guard at the Boyd home to protect the women.

Belle's spying career began when the first guard took his position. He—and the guards who would follow—liked to talk to this charming young woman, and Belle made the most of the opportunity. But Boyd was a little too obvious, and she drew attention to herself by her excessive curiosity. As a result, she was reported to authorities at least thirty times, brought in for questioning six times, and imprisoned twice before being sent into Confederate territory.

This does not mean, however, that Belle wasn't a successful spy. She regularly supplied General Stonewall Jackson with information, some of which she personally delivered. On one occasion, she claimed to have ridden into battle herself to give Jackson the information he needed to gain the advantage. And while attention was focused on her, it was drawn away from her spy ring of teenage girls, which operated over a large area and was, by all accounts, highly successful.

Boyd became ill during her second imprisonment, and in 1863 she decided to go to Europe for a rest. When she boarded the *Greyhound,* a blockade runner, she was carrying, in addition to her belongings, papers addressed to European leaders for President Jefferson Davis. The *Greyhound* was caught by Union patrol boats, and Belle, guilty of treason by Union standards, was taken to Boston, where she was to be imprisoned. She escaped from the naval officer who was assigned to guard her, Ensign Samuel Hardinge, and immediately headed to Canada. Belle then went on to London, where Hardinge joined her. They were married shortly after.

Like the North, the South was aided by many female spies. These included Laura Radcliffe of Virginia, Emeline Piggot of North Carolina, Rachel Mayer of South Carolina, and Isabella Brinsmade of Louisiana, all of whom were arrested and imprisoned. The Union was vigilant in trying to capture these "feminine desperadoes of the Confederacy," as they became known, and it arrested young and old alike. Even so, many of these clever women got away.

HARRIET TUBMAN

(c. 1821-1913)

Harriet Tubman is probably one of America's best known African-Americans. She was born into slavery on a plantation in Maryland. Harriet was beaten by her master when she was a child, and she was overworked in the fields as an adult. Defiant and proud, in 1849 Tubman made a courageous—and successful—dash for freedom.

Tubman dedicated the rest of her life to fighting slavery. She repeatedly returned to the South to lead other slaves to freedom. Each time she did so, she risked arrest. Nevertheless, she gladly helped more than 300 men, women, and children escape from their masters. Some of these former slaves settled in the North; others, with the help of the Underground Railroad, fled to Canada. Slave owners became so alarmed at Tubman's one-woman crusade that they offered a reward of $40,000 for her capture.

During the Civil War, Tubman worked as a nurse in the North as well as a spy behind Confederate lines— an incredibly dangerous activity for someone who was well known and openly sought.

After the war, she lived in Auburn, New York. With the help of a friend she wrote a book about her experiences, *Scenes in the Life of Harriet Tubman,* which was published in 1869.

CHAPTER FOUR

CARING FOR THE WOUNDED

The operation would begin, and in the midst of shrieks, curses, and wild laughs, the surgeon would wield over his wretched victim the glittering knife and saw; and soon the severed and ghastly limb, white as snow and spattered with blood, would fall upon the floor—one more added to the terrible pile.

Belle Reynolds, Union nurse

Anticipating a short, easy war, neither the North nor the South was prepared to care for a large number of injured soldiers in 1861. As a result, officials in Richmond had to scramble to find accommodations for the 1,600 wounded men brought into the city after the first major battle of the war, at Bull Run. When local hospitals were full, officials asked Richmonders to care for soldiers in their homes, and many agreed to do so. Medical students in a nearby school were brought in to dress wounds, and anyone who could cook was asked to provide food.

Meanwhile, Union doctors struggled to help their patients, most of whom were hospitalized in and around Washington. Volunteers helped the cause by going door-to-door to gather anything that could be used for bandages and slings—spare sheets, curtains, dresses, and petticoats—in a frantic attempt to increase medical supplies.

The shocking number of casualties in the first battle made both sides take a closer look at their medical corps, and what they found was unnerving at best. There were only thirty-eight doctors in both the North and the South who were trained to treat battle wounds. The Union Army had two horse-drawn ambulances fit for service and few medical tools that could be used to treat battlefield injuries; the Confederacy had even less.

Although both sides tried to build a well-supplied, adequately trained medical corps throughout the war, neither was ever really prepared to handle the number of casualties that resulted from a major battle in which thousands of men might be wounded in a single day. As a result, both corps were forced to use makeshift equipment. Old hotels and vacant buildings were turned into hospitals, and many surgeons performed amputations on an operating table that often was little more than a door suspended across two barrels. When chloroform, which was used to render patients unconscious, was in short supply, surgeons "fortified" soldiers who were scheduled for an amputation with whiskey. To keep them from screaming, patients were given bullets to bite on—thus the idiom "bite the bullet"—while the doctor cut and sawed.

The serious shortage of doctors put enormous pressure on the surgeons in the field. No physician could rest after a battle until all the wounded were treated. When the casualties numbered in the hundreds or thousands, it was not unusual for a doctor to operate until he collapsed. He was then revived and put back to work.

Because working for the medical corps was clearly demanding, both armies were reluctant to include women. Officials doubted that women could endure the rigors and horrors that they would face. Nurses would be subjected to long hours, difficult working conditions, the smell of festering wounds, and the sight of bleeding stumps where arms or legs had once been.

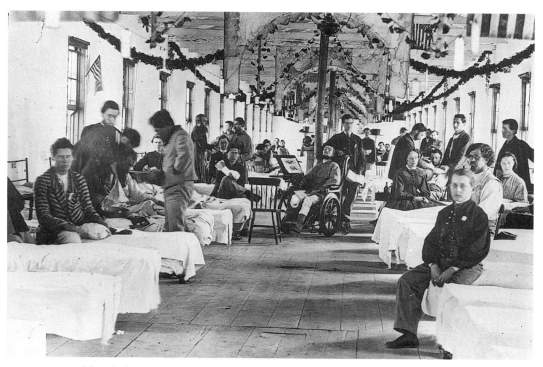

Although there was much resistance, no one could deny that the services of women were needed in hospitals during the Civil War, in both the North and the South. This hospital appears to be rather neat and orderly, but hospitals were usually understaffed and ill-equipped to deal with the huge number of casualties the battles produced.

Opponents also argued that caring for wounded soldiers was inappropriate for ladies. These officials pointed out that the war was being fought by all kinds of men, both heroes and ruffians, who might curse, make vulgar suggestions, and even assault comely nurses. Many would-be nurses, such as Julia Wheelock, considered this view of the army an insult to the "moral worth and true nobility of the soldier."[1] Even so, it was a commonly held belief.

Many also believed that it would be shocking for ladies to see men in various stages of undress, which tending some wounds would require. This belief was so strong that when

Elizabeth Blackwell, the first woman in America to receive a medical degree (1849), took courses at Geneva Medical College, she was required to leave the lecture hall when diagrams of male anatomy were shown. She sat outside the door and took notes the best she could from the comments she overheard in the classroom.

In addition, opponents of female nurses in the army pointed out, correctly, that few women had any formal training in nursing. There were exceptions, though: Several orders of Roman Catholic nuns, in both the North and the South, had been trained, but they specialized in home care, not battlefield wounds.

Those who called for women to be on staff in army hospitals reminded critics about the exceptional work done by Florence Nightingale, an English nurse, who cared for wounded soldiers in the Crimean War of 1853–1856. She had led thirty-eight women onto the battlefield to help the injured, heroes and ruffians alike. If she and her nurses could do it, supporters argued, so could American women.

Opponents could argue all they wanted, but they could not refuse to acknowledge the serious shortage of nurses that could be alleviated only by hiring women. So when women volunteered shortly after the war began, the troops accepted their help. Some nurses enlisted for patriotic reasons, while others wanted to help out of compassion for the wounded. More than a few enlisted for religious reasons, believing that they had been called by God to serve their countrymen. At least 3,000 women provided medical care at some time during the war.

Women in the North could become an army nurse in one of three ways. The easiest method was to join a local regiment when it organized, as a camp follower or a flag bearer might do. These positions were unofficial and lasted only as long as the regiment remained active.

Women also could join the Women's Central Relief Association in New York City, which was run by Dr. Elizabeth

Blackwell. Unlike other volunteers, Dr. Blackwell's nurses would receive professional training before they joined the soldiers.

Finally, would-be nurses could join a federally run organization headed by Dorothea Dix. She had made a reputation in the medical field by fighting for better living conditions and treatment for patients in mental institutions. Her successful campaign had required exceptional organizational skills and a determination to help others. So when, at the age of sixty, she volunteered her services in 1861, the Union accepted her help. Her program was under the watchful eye of the Union's surgeon general, Dr. William Hammond.

Dix was given an official military commission, command of all women who served in the Union's military hospitals, and the title Superintendent of Women Nurses. Although her nurses were supposed to remain in the Washington area and care only for the overflow of wounded that nurses in Northern regiments couldn't handle, the need for medical help in field hospitals near battlefields became so great that many nurses served there as well. Eventually Dix's corps, as well as Dr. Blackwell's, became part of the U.S. Sanitary Commission, which was in charge of all the medical programs of the Union Army.

Dorothea Dix, who personally interviewed every applicant for the military hospitals, was interested only in mature, serious, and respectable women in order to avoid any potential scandal or romantic entanglements. She announced: "No women under thirty need apply to serve in government hospitals. All nurses are required to be very plain looking. Nurses' dresses must be brown or black, with no bows, curls, jewelry and no hoop skirts."[2]

Even though applying meant admitting that they were plain looking, many women still wanted to join Dix's corps. To increase their chances of being hired, applicants brought a list of character references to their interview. Those who were hired were paid $12 per month. (Surgeons earned up to $150.)

Dix's nurses were trained in the hospitals where they were to serve, and they had little trouble finding something to do. Louisa May Alcott, before she became the well-known author of *Little Women*, worked as a nurse in the Union Hotel Hospital near Washington from late 1862 to early 1863, when she became seriously ill with typhoid fever. Alcott wrote about her experiences as a nurse in a book titled *Hospital Sketches:*

> Up at six, dress by gaslight, run through my ward and throw up the windows, though the men grumble and shiver; but the air is bad enough to breed a pestilence; and as no notice is taken of our frequent appeals for better ventilation, I must do what I can. Poke up the fire, add blankets, joke, coax, and command; but continue to open doors and windows as if life depended upon it. Mine does, and doubtless many another. . . . [3]

Then she and the other nurses went to work. They changed bandages and clothing, washed the men's hands and faces with strong brown soap, gave medications, and encouraged their patients to eat, and if possible, exercise. The Union Hotel Hospital held about 200 patients.

Alcott complained about the living conditions in the hotel, but by the time she arrived on the scene, this hospital was in far better shape than it had been. The improvement was due to the unrelenting efforts of Hannah Ropes.

Ropes had become a supervisor in the hospital in July 1862. Previously, she had been one of many Yankee settlers in Kansas. Hannah, her son, and her daughter had rushed into the territory to strengthen anti-slavery forces there when Congress gave the citizens in the territory the right to vote on the slavery issue in 1854. Ropes had read Florence Nightingale's book about nursing, *Notes on Nursing: What It Is, and What It Is Not,* and when war broke out she decided to serve in a military hospital.

She then traveled to Washington, DC, and shortly after, she was hired by Dorothea Dix.

Ropes was shocked by what she found in the Union Hotel, especially the filth and the stench from old, unchanged bandages. Believing that the actions of the head surgeon and one of his assistants were harmful to the patients, she took her case to the surgeon general. When he refused to listen to her, Hannah went directly to the secretary of war, Edwin Stanton, which was a gutsy thing to do. Stanton ordered an investigation, and when all the facts were known, the surgeon and his assistant were arrested for abusing their patients. Ropes continued to make improvements in the hospital (such as providing more food for the injured) until her death in 1863 from typhoid fever, which she had contracted in the hospital.

Ropes wasn't the only nurse to challenge authority. Quite a few female nurses at one time or another were unwilling to blindly follow a doctor's orders. This was the result of Dorothea Dix's hiring practices and the medical corps' push to put as many doctors into the field as soon as possible, ready or not. Dix had hired mature women who, if they were to survive in their positions, had to be confident and strong. Also, many of these nurses, especially those in their forties and fifties, had had more experience caring for sick patients, friends, and relatives at home than many of the young doctors. So when the nurses saw something that they thought was wrong, they were not afraid to stand up to their superiors or do what they thought was best.

As rebellion among the nurses became more common, some surgeons tried to avoid problems by not having women on their medical staffs at all. When the Union's surgeon general insisted that at least one-third of all nursing positions in military hospitals be given to women, some doctors tried to fill their quota with nuns because they were more likely to take orders.

The Union nurse who probably held the record for doing things her own way was Mary Bickerdyke. Mother Bickerdyke, as she was commonly known, was a widow in her mid-forties. When she was placed in charge of the military hospitals in Cairo, Illinois, she quickly turned the chaotic hospitals into well-run institutions. She ordered every able-bodied person available to scrub the wards, clean the kitchens, and restock the pantries with ample supplies of food. She even ordered officers and surgeons about. She did so much to help the soldiers that they and their officers considered her the most important person in the army.

Although the soldiers appreciated Mother Bickerdyke, some of the surgeons did not. When she decided to attend a doctor during an operation, the surgeon demanded to know who gave her permission to do so. She replied, "I am present on the authority of the Lord God Almighty. Have you anything that outranks that?"[4] The surgeon did not reply, and Bickerdyke remained.

In another incident, Mother Bickerdyke accused one of the surgeons of misconduct. The surgeon then appealed directly to General Ulysses S. Grant for help. When Grant heard the surgeon's story, he refused to support him, warning the doctor that "Mother Bickerdyke outranks everybody, even Lincoln. If you have run amuck of her I advise you to get out quickly before she has you under arrest."[5]

While Mother Bickerdyke was shaping up Cairo's military hospitals, Dr. Mary Walker was struggling to get permission to serve in the army at all. Deeply patriotic and seeing the war as a chance to prove that female physicians could serve on the battlefield, Walker went to Washington shortly after the war started to offer her services. She was rejected because officials thought that it was unnatural for a woman to supervise the health care of men, which included diagnosing illnesses, recommending surgery, or even more shocking, actually performing the surgery.

This picture of Mary "Mother" Bickerdyke, a well-known and respected nurse for the Union, was taken later in her life. General Grant said of her, "Mother Bickerdyke outranks everybody, even Lincoln."

Determined to serve and prove her worth, Dr. Walker volunteered to work with the Army of the Potomac. She traveled about, showing up at battle sites where doctors were so overwhelmed with injured men that the surgeons had no choice but to accept her help. When the patients were stabilized, she accompanied the wounded on a train to military hospitals. Once her charges were safe and comfortable, Walker headed back to the battlefields.

Dr. Preston King had worked beside Walker, and he was greatly impressed with her medical expertise. When he learned that she was receiving no pay, only room and board for her extraordinary work, he petitioned Secretary of War Edwin Stanton, asking him to compensate Walker for what she had done. But Stanton refused to do so, arguing that only those commissioned could receive pay.

Walker's volunteer work continued until 1864, when emboldened by her many contacts and growing reputation, she decided to seek an appointment through President Lincoln. She listed where she had served and what she had accomplished, closing her letter by saying: "Had a man been as useful to our country as [I] modestly claim to have been, a star would have been taken from the National Heavens and placed upon his shoulder."[6] But it was no use—Lincoln, bowing to the army's doctors, who were opposed to her candidacy, refused her an appointment.

It was General George Thomas who came to her aid. He told her to stop trying to get an appointment in a military hospital. Instead, like some of the nurses, she should offer her services to a regiment. Dr. Walker followed his advice and, shortly after, began to work as a full-fledged surgeon in Ohio.

The Confederate Medical Corps was led by Dr. Samuel Preston Moore. This corps was even more adamant in refusing to let women serve as army surgeons than was the North. Any woman attempting to do so—at least two female physicians were serving in the South then—would have faced even more resistance than Dr. Mary Walker did, as well as overwhelming public condemnation, as Walker suffered when she was captured by Southern soldiers.

At this time, Dr. Walker was serving in southern Ohio. On a rare day during which her skills were not urgently needed, she decided to take a break and go horseback riding. She was unfamiliar with the area and eventually strayed into Confederate territory.

Walker was soon spotted by Southern scouts, who arrested her and took her to a nearby camp for questioning. The fact that she was wearing trousers caused as much commotion in the camp as did the rumor that the scouts had caught a female spy. When the soldiers found out that Walker was serving as a surgeon, they could hardly contain themselves.

Confederate Captain B.J. Semmes spoke for many when, after studying Walker, he gave his scathing reaction to her in a letter to a friend:

> This morning we were all amused and disgusted too at the sight of a thing that nothing but the debased and the depraved Yankee nation could produce—a female doctor. . . . She was dressed in the full uniform of a Federal Surgeon. . . [She is] fair, but not good looking and of course had tongue enough for a regiment of men. I was in hopes that the General [Joseph E. Johnston] would have had her dressed in a homespun frock and bonnet and sent back to the Yankee lines, or put in a lunatic asylum. . . .[7]

When Walker was taken to Richmond to be imprisoned, curious Southerners lined the city's streets to get a glimpse of the strange Yankee. Gawkers sneered and snickered and shouted insults as she passed by.

Although serving as an army surgeon was not acceptable in the South, women were welcome in Southern hospitals, both as nurses and administrators. However, there was no organized program to put them there, such as Dorothea Dix's in the North. Instead, many nurses simply volunteered their services. Those who owned slaves often brought them along to help.

Working conditions in Confederate hospitals, like those on the Union side, were far from perfect. Kate Cumming, who served near Corinth, Mississippi, began her work in the Tishomingo Hotel, which, like every other large building in the area, was being used as a hospital.

The scenes that greeted Southern nurses were no less traumatic than those witnessed by their counterparts in the North. Cumming recalled:

> Mrs. Ogden tried to prepare me for the scenes which I should witness upon entering the wards. But alas! nothing that I had ever heard or read had given me the faintest idea of the horrors witnessed here. . . . Gray-haired men, men in the pride of manhood, beardless boys, federals and all, mutilated in every imaginable way, lying on the floor, just as they were taken from the battlefield; so close together that it was almost impossible to walk without stepping on them. I could not command my feelings enough to speak.[8]

Like Kate, Ella King Newsom began her medical career with the Confederate Army as a nurse. A wealthy widow from Arkansas, Newsom first cared for wounded soldiers in Bowling Green, Kentucky, in late 1861. Her work so impressed her superiors that she was asked to run all the military hospitals in the city. Later, she served in Chattanooga, Tennessee, and Atlanta, Georgia.

Sally Tompkins established her own hospital in Richmond. Shortly after the battle at Bull Run, she turned an old mansion into Robertson Hospital, where she, her four slaves, and a large crew of volunteers cared for more than 1,300 soldiers during the war. President Jefferson Davis was so pleased with her work that he made her a captain in the Confederate Army, the only woman to receive such an honor.

Phoebe Yates Pember also worked in a Southern hospital. A young widow from a respectable family, Pember left her home in Charleston for Richmond as soon as war broke out, hoping to nurse the wounded there. She eventually became a superintendent of Chimborazo, a large hospital on the outskirts of the city. Part of her staff included six female slaves, who were paid, although their salaries were turned over to their owners.

As the war dragged on, the Confederate armies were forced to retreat more often. This posed serious problems for the wounded soldiers and their nurses. The Army of Tennessee retreated four times, and nurse Kate Cumming moved her patients each time. Often the nurses commandeered wagons for the weakest patients, packed the medications, and prepared food for the flight southward. If patients were too weak to be moved, then the nurses, such as Fannie Beers, remained behind to care for the men, knowing full well that by doing so they risked capture.

As the casualties mounted and more help was needed, hospitals in Richmond even sought the help of free blacks, both men and women, to nurse the wounded. Many hospitals offered room and board in addition to wages to entice applicants.

By far, the largest number of wounded soldiers in the North and South were cared for in private homes either by female family members or townspeople who were willing to help. The names of these women do not appear in hospital or army records, nor were the women ever given special medals or national recognition. But their unheralded work saved thousands of lives.

Clara Harlowe Barton
(1821-1912)

Clara Harlowe Barton was working in the patent office in Washington, when the first wounded soldiers were brought into the city. Like many other volunteers, she rushed to local hospitals to care for the injured men. Shortly after, she applied for—and received—permission to go to the front to work as a nurse.

Clara began her work by setting up a tent near Cedar Mountain in Virginia, where a battle had just taken place. She accepted wounded and dying soldiers from both sides.

Later, Barton traveled with the Union Army to nurse the wounded, find supplies, and search for the missing. She was especially good at tracking down the whereabouts or remains of missing soldiers. Even so, toward the end of the war, at least 60,000 Union soldiers were still unaccounted for, and their families wanted information on their status. President Lincoln then asked Clara to take on the enormous task of finding the missing men. She studied hospital and prisoner-of-war records and searched graveyards near battlefields for clues. Eventually she was able to account for 30,000 of the soldiers in question.

Clara Barton went to Europe in 1869 to do similar work in the Franco-Prussian War with the International Red Cross. She returned to the United States in 1873, and founded the American National Red Cross in 1881.

CHAPTER FIVE

As First Ladies

Mary, Mary, we are elected!

> Abraham Lincoln,
> President-Elect of the United States

During the Civil War, few women received more attention than did Mary Todd Lincoln and Varina Howell Davis, first ladies of their respective countries. The public scrutinized the women's activities, statements, and clothing, and described in detail what had been seen and heard at social gatherings and in newspapers of the day. Not all the comments about the women were kind, for both first ladies became scapegoats, people upon whom the public could heap its anger and frustration as the war dragged on.

Each first lady tried to ignore her critics and attempted to run her country's White House as efficiently as possible. The vast majority of each wife's time, however, was spent on efforts to protect and support her husband. The results of these efforts were quite different: One first lady became so overwhelmed by her burdens that she sometimes teetered on the brink of an emotional breakdown; the other showed amazing strength and courage, becoming stronger as the war progressed.

Even though she was a bright and well-educated woman, the fact that her husband came from humble beginnings and had no prominent ancestors made many believe that Mary Todd Lincoln lacked the social skills necessary to be a proper First Lady. And since she was sensitive to criticism, sparks often flew between Mary and the socialites of Washington.

Mary Todd Lincoln was considered unfit for her position as First Lady of the United States by many Americans who chose to ignore her background and achievements. Mary was born in 1818 in Lexington, Kentucky, which was considered little more than a frontier town by Eastern society. She was the daughter of Robert and Eliza Parker Todd. The prosperous Todd family included politicians and wealthy merchants.

Mary's mother died while giving birth to her seventh child. Mr. Todd married Elizabeth Humphreys shortly after, and they had nine children. The Todd home was large enough to accommodate this many children, even though they were, by all reports, spirited and rambunctious. The household was maintained by servants and slaves.

Mary was bright and well educated. She attended an exclusive finishing school, which specialized in educating young ladies in music, literature, and French—with a Parisian accent. Madame Mentelle, the headmistress, also taught her students social skills, including the fine points of letter writing and carrying on interesting conversations.

Because Mary excelled in school and was pretty and lively, her parents believed that she, like the other Todds, would marry well. As a result, her father and stepmother were stunned when Mary decided to marry Abraham Lincoln, whom she had met while visiting her sister and brother-in-law in Springfield, Illinois. The Todds were openly dismayed by Lincoln's lack of education and wealth as well as his lack of distinguished ancestors. But Mary and Abe had many things in common, including a deep interest in politics, and their marriage was a happy one, even though the Todds thought that Lincoln was "a hard bargain."

Many Republicans from socially prominent families also considered Lincoln a hard bargain, as was any woman who would marry him. One senator's wife summed up the socialites' beliefs in her journal shortly after the president-elect, Mary, and

Robert, the Lincolns' oldest son, arrived in Washington. (Two younger sons, Tad and Willie, would join them later.) "[Brewster] says he hears from all quarters that the vulgarity of Lincoln, his wife, and his son is beyond credence—a thing you must see before you can believe it."[1]

Because Mary was thought to be lacking the necessary social graces to be a good First Lady, several wives of well-known Republican senators called upon her shortly after her arrival to give her some tips on entertaining. Mary was extremely sensitive to criticism, and she had quite a temper as well. She let the women know in no uncertain terms that she could handle the position without their help. It was but one of many displays of anger that gave Mary's critics another item to add to their list of her faults.

Not only was Mary's social know-how challenged, so was her loyalty to the Union. Her critics pointed out that she was a member of a Southern family and that her brother, half-brothers, and most of her brothers-in-law were fighting for the Confederacy. Rumormongers said that Mary was a Southern spy. They even insisted that they had seen suspicious characters climbing down ladders from the First Lady's window in the White House with messages in hand for the Confederacy.

Mary's role became crucial when war was declared shortly after Lincoln took office. A White House reception, complete with fine wines and a gourmet dinner, went a long way toward easing the many tensions that existed between members of Congress and President Lincoln as the men struggled over how best to win the war. In addition, entertaining European representatives in the White House was a way to gain support for the Union. Some historians believe that the favorable impression that Mary made on the French Prince Bonaparte when he visited Washington in 1861 helped to persuade France not to support the Confederacy during the conflict.

All the parties and dinners cost a lot of money, though, and Mary, who was eager to impress, ran up large debts. She redecorated the White House, which had become shabby and worn, to provide the perfect setting for her receptions. Congress agreed to spend $20,000 to update the mansion; Mary spent $27,000. Mary tried to raise the extra $7,000 by diverting funds from an unfilled staff position to the White House's budget. But this highly questionable effort was unsuccessful. Eventually, her overspending came to light, and her critics reacted with howls of protest. When she cut back on entertaining to please her critics, however, they called her a tightwad.

Mary refused to defend herself, arguing that any statements on her part would only make things worse. Instead, she concentrated on helping her husband. She made every effort to see that the president ate well, taking meals to him in his office when he was too busy to go to the dining room for lunch. She also insisted that he take breaks, some of which included carriage rides in the fresh air and sunshine. And she read as many newspapers and journals of the day as possible, summarizing them for the president to keep him up-to-date on all events in the country.

Mary was also free with her advice on how to win the war. This brought her into conflict with members of the president's cabinet, who often referred to her as the "lady-president" behind her back.

When time permitted, Mary helped wounded soldiers. She visited local hospitals, often with a basket of baked goods and fresh fruit, gave the men some of her own money, and raised funds for their medical care. Mary did not always identify herself, and her good deeds often went unnoticed.

The First Lady was also a devoted mother. Because she had already lost one son, Eddie, long before the Lincoln family moved to Washington, Mary was especially protective of her remaining three boys. When eleven-year-old Willie became seriously ill early in 1862, Mary was nearly hysterical. When he died on February 20, she became so emotionally unstable that the president feared that she would end up in a mental institution. With the help of friends and family, Mary struggled hard to regain control of her emotions, fearing that to fail to do so would hinder the president and the war effort. It took all the courage that she could muster, though. Later she recalled, "If I had not felt the spur of necessity urging me to cheer Mr. Lincoln, whose grief was as great as my own, I could never have smiled again."[2]

By the time her husband was elected to a second term in 1864, Mary's emotional well-being was in doubt. She indulged in extravagant shopping sprees between debilitating headaches that forced her to take to bed for days at a time. Fearing for her husband's life after reading some of the death threats that arrived daily, she was suspicious of almost everyone who entered the White House.

When General Robert E. Lee surrendered on April 9, 1865, Mary, like most Americans, was overwhelmed with relief. Believing that her worst nightmares were behind her, she decided that she and the president should celebrate by attending a play at Ford's Theatre. On April 14, Mary sat beside her husband in a private box overlooking the stage. Suddenly a man named John Wilkes Booth pushed open the door to the box and fatally shot the president.

The shock and horror of the event sent Mary reeling. For days, she sobbed uncontrollably or prayed that she would die then and there. She was even too distraught to attend her husband's funeral. About a month later, no longer a first lady, Mary left the White House and moved to Chicago with her two sons. Her role in the Civil War was over.

Although the results were quite different, Varina Howell Davis's experiences as First Lady were strangely similar to those of Mary Todd Lincoln. Like Mary, Varina was consid-

Since there had been no First Lady of the Confederacy before her to set a precedent, Varina Howell Davis had to make her own rules—and gained her share of critics in the process. This picture of her and Jefferson Davis, her husband and president of the Confederacy, was taken shortly after their marriage in 1845.

ered unfit to be the First Lady of her country because she, too, was from a frontier state. Varina was born in 1826 in Natchez, Mississippi, the daughter of William and Margaret Kempe Howell. Varina's ancestors included Revolutionary War heroes and wealthy plantation owners.

And like Mary, Varina was well educated. At first, she was tutored at home by a family friend, Judge George Winchester, a graduate of Harvard who lived with the Howells in Natchez. Varina adored the judge, and she credited him with teaching her the most important lessons of her life. "The most valuable lessons I learned were not from the Latin or English classics... but from the pure high standard of right, of which his course was the exemplar."[3] When Varina was ten years old, she was enrolled in Madame Grelaud's school in Philadelphia.

Varina met Jefferson Davis, a young widower, when she visited family friends in southern Mississippi, where Davis had a plantation called Brierfield. They were married shortly afterward.

Jefferson Davis was deeply involved in politics, and Varina became a devoted political wife. Davis was elected to the U.S. House of Representatives in 1845 and the U.S. Senate in 1847. He also served as secretary of war under President Franklin Pierce (1853–1857), then returned to the Senate until Mississippi seceded from the Union. When Jefferson Davis was chosen as president of the Confederacy by the delegates of the seceded states, Varina followed him to Montgomery, Alabama, where a temporary capital had been established. She had barely gotten unpacked when the capital was moved to Richmond, Virginia.

Varina had many critics to deal with. She had few rules or traditions on which she could rely, for she was the first woman to occupy the South's White House. To avoid offending anyone, Varina held open houses. These receptions were popular, but they had to be abandoned as the war progressed. Many threats were made on President Davis's life, and it became too dangerous to allow anyone to enter the White House unchecked and unrestricted.

Varina also held formal receptions. At first, these parties weren't elaborate enough for some of Richmond's elite society; later, when the South was suffering serious setbacks and supplies were hard to come by, such receptions were thought to be too elaborate by the same critics.

Varina's main role, however, like Mary Lincoln's, was to support her husband. President Davis faced overwhelming responsibilities. He had to build a government from scratch and lead a war at the same time. In addition, Jefferson Davis's health was poor, in large part due to the stresses he endured while in the U.S. Senate where he repeatedly tried to work out compromises to prevent the South's secession. He suffered from facial neuralgia, a painful affliction of the nerve endings. He was also blind in one eye, and frequent infections threatened his remaining vision. Varina took it upon herself to make sure that he ate and rested. When he was overwhelmed with problems, especially toward the end of the war, she read to him to give him something to think about for a little while besides war, death, and defeat.

Varina also screened an unending parade of people who wanted to see the president. She sent away anyone who could find the answer to his or her questions somewhere else. And she often listened to pleas for help herself, summarized them briefly, and then presented them to her husband on the visitors' behalf.

In addition, Varina was a busy mother. The Davises had three children when the war began. Two more children were born in the White House. Like the Lincolns, the Davises had lost their first child, a son, before Davis became president. And like the Lincolns, the Davises would lose another child in the White House. On April 30, 1864, five-year-old Joe fell to his death from an upstairs White House balcony.

Although Washington, the Union capital, was threatened by the Confederates early in the war, it wasn't in serious danger throughout most of the conflict. Capturing the Confederate capital of Richmond, on the other hand, was a major goal of Union troops, and this city faced the constant threat of invasion. The First Lady often heard gunfire as Union troops advanced, sometimes to within 3 miles (5 kilometers) of the city's outskirts.

Whenever President Davis thought that the Confederate lines protecting the city might break, he insisted that Varina take the children and retreat to safer ground. This resulted in intense criticism of Varina. One Southern woman, Catherine Edmonston, wrote in her diary: "Mrs. Davis has left Richmond and gone to Raleigh, fairly deserted her colors. I fear she is not a woman of the true stamp. I fear she does not strengthen her husband, or she would never have abandoned her post & set such an example to the rest of the women of the Confederacy." One week later, still upset by Mrs. Davis's departure, Edmonston wrote: "Mrs. Davis is, I hear, a Philadelphia woman! That accounts for . . . her flight from Richmond."[4]

After failing to take Richmond in a major drive in 1862, Union forces lay siege to the city, attempting to cut off all supplies entering the capital and starve the city into submission. This made running the White House extremely difficult since the scarcity of supplies drove prices sky-high: By early 1863, a large ham cost $350, and sugar was $12 a pound. Varina struggled to find adequate foodstuffs for her parties and receptions, which she felt had to go on. She was simply unwilling to abandon dances for returning soldiers and army officers, believing that some show of support and appreciation was absolutely necessary.

As the South lost more and more battles—even the Davis' home in Mississippi had been taken by the middle of 1863—it became more difficult than ever to keep the White House running smoothly. Servants were bribed by Union supporters in Richmond to leave the city to create disorder. Whether Elizabeth Van Lew's spy in the White House tried to stir up trouble while she gathered information is not certain, but her dedication to the Union was so great that it's hard to believe that she didn't seize every opportunity to further her cause.

By early 1865, the Confederacy was under enormous pressure by General Grant's troops to surrender. President Davis refused to do so; instead, he made plans to move the Confederate government, and his family, to safety—perhaps as far away as Texas. On April 2, General Robert E. Lee informed President Davis that the Confederate Army could no longer protect Richmond. Jefferson then told Varina, who was determined to remain by her husband's side, that she and the children had to leave. Varina reluctantly and tearfully agreed to go, knowing that she might never again see her husband. "With hearts bowed down by despair," she wrote later, "we left Richmond."[5]

Varina was supposed to go to the coast of Florida, where, if necessary, she could make arrangements to flee to Europe. She rode part of the way on the train that carried the Confederacy's treasury from Richmond. When the train broke down, her party of family members, servants, and guards traveled in wagons and on horseback through miles of wilderness, trying to remain out of sight as much as possible. They received little help, since most Southerners were afraid that the Union troops, who were expected shortly, would punish them if they aided the First Lady in any way.

Varina and Jefferson meant to travel separately, but their paths crossed in Georgia, less than 100 miles (160 kilometers) from the Florida border. Concerned for his family's safety when he heard that thieves were looking for the treasury, Jefferson Davis had turned around and headed east to protect Varina and the children.

The Davises had been together only a few days before Union troops surrounded them near Irwinville, Georgia. On May 10, President Davis was arrested. He was accused of being part of the plot to kill President Lincoln and confined to Fortress Monroe near Richmond to await trial. Varina was held in Savannah in a small hotel for a while.

When she was finally released, Varina began a successful two-year battle to secure her husband's release from prison. Unlike Mary Todd Lincoln, Varina still had a public role to play, and for her the Civil War was far from finished.

Julia Gardiner Tyler
First Lady, 1844-45

During the Civil War, attention was also focused on former First Ladies and their roles in the war. Julia Gardiner Tyler was of special interest because her husband, John Tyler, the tenth president of the United States and a native of Virginia, was a strong supporter of secession. Tyler, who served in the Confederate Congress, died in 1862.

Julia Tyler, a native of Gardiners Island, New York, became concerned about her mother's safety back in New York once John Tyler's part in Virginia's secession became known. Julia had learned that some of her Northern relatives had been threatened, and several had been forced to flee for their lives. In 1863 she decided to go to New York to protect her mother.

While Julia was living in the North, she continued to support the Confederacy. She helped the Copperheads, a group of Northern Democrats who demanded an immediate end to the war, which would have resulted in the South's independence. Julia also bought Confederate bonds, distributed anti-Lincoln pamphlets in New York, and sent money and clothes to Confederate soldiers. Her involvement did little to endear her to Northerners, but this did not matter to Julia. Her love for the Confederacy was deep and undying.

CHAPTER SIX ∽

WITH PEN IN HAND

Woman has now taken to her pen . . . and is flourishing it with a vengeance.

Leslie's Illustrated Newspaper

During the Civil War, women often took to their pens, and they had many experiences about which they could write. They recorded their activities in journals, wrote stories and patriotic songs that many Americans still sing today, and created a stir with petitions.

The majority of women who wrote during this period did so in journals. Although more than a hundred of these would eventually be published, providing valuable eyewitness accounts of what life was like at the time, most women considered their entries personal and meant for their eyes only.

Sixteen-year-old Clara Solomon of New Orleans began her journal on June 15, 1861, about two months after the war began. Her first entry shows her enthusiasm and attention to detail:

"10 3/4 A.M. At last, have I commenced my new book. How long it has been in expectation, I need not say. But I did really think that this moment would never arrive."[1]

Clara recorded the comings and goings of family members and the dreaded arrival of the Yankees. Unable to do anything to stop the enemy, the Solomon family used every means it had to pester Union troops, including the provision of an ample supply of mosquitoes. On May 17, 1862, Clara wrote: "Endeavored to kill as few mosquitoes as possible. For two reasons, the first being that we should be polluted by being touched by Yankee blood, & secondly, each one increases the number & aids in biting & tormenting [Yankees]. I wonder how they like them!"[2]

Sometimes women used information from their journals in writing their memoirs or as a background for their novels. Publication was possible, since women authors had already been well accepted long before the war began. Harriet Beecher Stowe, for example, sold more than 300,000 copies of her novel *Uncle Tom's Cabin* in 1852, the first year that it appeared in print. Throughout the war, there was a strong demand for novels about the conflict. Editors eagerly sought stories, and women happily provided the manuscripts.

Memoirs, especially in the South, became the rage of the day. When Confederate women encountered difficulty in getting published as the South's supply of paper and ink dwindled, the writers sought other places for publication. Spies Rose O'Neal Greenhow and Belle Boyd, for example, had their manuscripts published in England. Greenhow's book, *My Imprisonment and the First Year of the Abolition Rule in Washington,* described her ordeal under house arrest. Boyd's book, *Belle Boyd in Camp and Prison,* is so incredible that most historians consider it little more than fiction. However, it was a popular book.

Spies were not the only Confederate women to publish books during or after the war. Many Southern women published firsthand accounts and novels. These included *A Journal of Hospital Life in the Confederate Army* by Kate Cumming and *A Southern Woman's Story* by Phoebe Yates Pember. One of the most famous Confederate novelists of the war was Augusta Jane Evans, who published *Altars of Sacrifice* in 1863. This novel presented the Confederacy's cause so well that the book was banned in Union camps.

Not to be outdone by Southern spies, Union spy Pauline Cushman published a book about her espionage activities, *The Thrilling Adventures of Pauline Cushman*. The book, which first appeared in 1864, was a success, and it generated so much curiosity about the spy-actress that people flocked to the theater to see her in person.

Cushman was only one of many Northern women who published firsthand accounts. Most of the books, however, appeared after the war ended. These included *Three Years in the Field Hospitals of the Army of the Potomac* by Anna Morris Ellis Holstein, *A Woman's Life Work* by Laura Haviland, and *In Hospital and Camp* by Sophronia Bucklin.

Women found that one of the most profitable areas of publishing, though, was sheet music. By 1861 more than 20,000 pianos were being manufactured in the United States each year. This alone created a great demand for musical scores. When the war began, the demand soared; both sections wanted new songs for patriotic programs, parades, and family gatherings, where members often stood around a piano and sang.

The "Battle Hymn of the Republic," a poem written by Julia Ward Howe, became the unofficial song of the Union. Howe wrote the words, which were sung to a popular melody of the day, after a visit to a Union camp near Washington in late 1861. It was only one of many poems that she wrote about the conflict, but it was by far her most popular piece. For the rest of her life, she was hounded by admirers seeking autographed copies of the song.

"Somebody's Darling" by Marie Ravenal de la Coste was the most popular song written by a Southern woman during the war. She was inspired to write the words after visiting a

In the 1860s, sheet music, to be played on the piano, was the way people brought music into their homes. Songs relating to the war were especially popular. The sad song "Somebody's Darling," with lyrics written by Marie Ravenal de la Coste, was one of the best-sellers.

Confederate hospital, where she saw many young men near death, each one someone's son. The emotional song, especially the chorus ("Somebody's darling, somebody's pride, who'll tell his mother where her boy died?"[3]) struck a chord with Northerners and Southerners alike. This song was so popular that printers couldn't keep up with the demand. Years later, it was thought to be so typical of the period that it was included in the sound track of *Gone with the Wind,* a famous film about the Civil War.

Women also found publication opportunities in the more than 600 magazines of the day. However, the most influential women's magazine, *Godey's Lady's Book,* refused to take any manuscripts that discussed or even hinted at political issues. *Godey's* even refused to let Dr. Elizabeth Blackwell publish a letter asking readers to enlist in the war effort as nurses. As a result, the editor, Sarah Hale, was roundly criticized. In fact, the magazine's no-politics stand so angered the public that 30 percent of its readers dropped their subscriptions during the war.

Other magazines were not afraid to discuss the war, though, or to give support to one side or another. One of the most powerful pleas to appear in a periodical during the Civil War was written by Mary Abigail Dodge. Titled "A Call to My Country-women," it was published in the *Atlantic Monthly* in early 1863, when it seemed as if the war-weary North might lose the conflict simply because it appeared to lack the will to win. Dodge asked Northern women to dry their tears, stop their fretting, and start setting an example. Women, she said, had to be stronger and more cheerful in order to improve the soldiers' morale if the conflict was to be won by the Union. This essay was one of the most discussed pieces in print during the war.

Newspapers routinely covered the conflict, giving readers as much information about the war as they could. To encourage women to read newspapers, some editors hired female reporters. Although most of these reporters covered traditionally female beats, such as fashion and household hints, a few wrote about political issues.

One of the best-known wartime reporters was Jane Grey Swisshelm. Swisshelm was an abolitionist, one of the first female reporters to work for Horace Greeley's *New York Tribune,* the first woman to sit in the Senate press gallery in Washington, and an outspoken critic of hoop skirts and corsets. When the war broke out, she was working for the *Democrat,* a paper in St. Cloud, Minnesota. Strong-willed and opinionated, Jane had antagonized local politicians. One of them, James Shepley, gave a public speech that attacked "strong-minded women." Everyone knew that Shepley was talking about Swisshelm, including Jane, and she responded by giving lectures of her own—about the role of women as she saw it.

Jane traveled to Washington to cover the war. Although she discussed the events of the conflict in general, she concentrated on stories about the troops from Minnesota. She encouraged readers to ship blankets, soap, and clothing to the soldiers, and discouraged the popular practice of sending red hats, which made the men easy targets.

Swisshelm also worked as a volunteer in Union hospitals. When she noticed lice in the beds of one hospital, she lambasted authorities—in print—accusing them of running slipshod institutions. Jane was relieved of her nursing duties shortly after. She noted, however, "Nobody denied the truth of my statements about Douglas Hospital, and I never learned that any one objected to the facts . . . . It was only their exposure which gave offense."[4]

During the war, a large number of suffragists, many of whom were abolitionists as well, also put their pens to work.

Because winning the war did not guarantee freedom for the slaves—President Lincoln had long insisted that it was a war to keep the Union together, not to abolish slavery—these women believed that an amendment to the U.S. Constitution was needed to achieve that goal. In 1863 they met in New York to form the Women's National Loyal League. This league, which included leading suffragists of the day, such as Susan B. Anthony, Elizabeth Cady Stanton, and Lucy Stone, decided to put aside the demand for the vote for the duration of the war and concentrate on abolition. The women then organized a petition drive to compel state and national leaders to draft and ratify an anti-slavery amendment.

With pens in hand, the women set out to get every signature that they could. This campaign proved to be the most successful petition drive in the history of the abolition movement, securing more than 400,000 names. It also gave many women experience in organizing a petition drive and speaking out for a cause. As a result, many became seasoned fighters who were ready to push ahead for suffrage after the war.

Mary Chesnut's Journal

One of the most famous journals of the Civil War was written by a South Carolinian, Mary Boykin Chesnut (1823–1886). Mary was the daughter of a wealthy plantation owner and the wife of James Chesnut, a former U.S. senator and an aide to President Jefferson Davis. Mary's journal included heartbreaking scenes she had witnessed during the war, her opinion of Confederate leaders (not always good), her activities with dear friends, including Varina Davis, and her hopes for her country. She was a smart, lively, outspoken woman, as even a few entries will prove:

Christmas Day, 1863. Yesterday dined at the Prestons with one of my handsomest Paris dresses (from Paris before the war). Three magnificent Kentucky generals. Orr, senator from S.C., and Mr. Miles. . . . We had for dinner oyster soup . . . boiled mutton, ham, boned turkey, wild ducks, partridges, plum pudding . . . burgundy, sherry, and Madeira wine.

There is life in the old land yet!

And now for our Christmas dinner. We invited two wounded homeless men who were too ill to come. Alex Haskell, however, who has lost an eye, and Hood came. . . . My dinner was comparatively a simple affair—oysters, ham, turkey, partridges, and good wine.

December 26, 1863. [My son] said I was extravagant. . . . He called me "hospitality run mad.". . . We are all busy looking after poor soldiers' wives. . . . There are no end of them here. And they never have less than nine or ten children. . . . The whole duty here consists in abusing Lincoln and the Yankees [and] praising Jeff Davis and the Army of Virginia. And wondering when this horrid war will be over.

There is not one of us who seems to believe for a moment that we will ever again have an ache or a pain or a trouble or a care, if peace were once proclaimed and a triumphant Southern Confederacy [could wave] its flag in defiance of the world. What geese we are![5]

CHAPTER SEVEN

ON THE HOME FRONT

O women, the hour has need of you.

Mary Abigail Dodge,
Northern author

Women on the home front in the North and South were eager to help their side. The opportunity to do so and the problems they faced varied greatly, however, from one section to the other.

From the beginning, the North was better able to fight an all-out war than was the South. The North had a population of 22 million; the South had 9 million people, including 3.5 million slaves. In addition, just before the war started, the North was producing nine-tenths of the nation's industrial goods and two-thirds of the country's food. The North also had two-thirds of America's railroad tracks and a vast array of resources from which to draw.

Once the war began, the Union grew even stronger. The government needed uniforms, tents, munitions, and foodstuffs, and industry, workers, and farmers not only were able to fill federal orders, but their expanding businesses also produced surpluses, which were sold abroad. The growing economy attracted thousands of immigrants. As a result, even though the war claimed the lives of many men, the North actually had more people at the end of the bloody conflict than it did in 1860.

Because the North had so many workers, there was not a heavy demand for female employees when the war began. But as government orders increased during the conflict, more workers were needed to fill the requests. As a result, some women were hired. By 1865, approximately 270,000 women—still less than 2 percent of the adult females in the North—were employed in industry.

Even though there was great concern about women working outside the home where they could not be protected from the so-called wicked world, employers actually preferred to hire single women. (Married women were expected to remain at home.) Unlike many men, single women had no families to support and were willing to work for low wages. In addition, many women had been taught how to weave and sew at home, and the textile and garment industries, the major employers of women, did not have to spend a lot of time teaching them how to do their jobs.

Shirts were made in homes as well by poor married women, who then sold the garments to the government. As the war dragged on, more women, many of whom were widowed by the conflict, joined this effort.

Union women also helped supply the government through aid societies scattered all across the North. Volunteers met in homes and churches, and many sites became well-run workshops. Women knit socks, rolled bandages, packed baskets of foodstuffs, and made uniforms and shirts.

The combined production systems—industrial, home-based, and volunteer—resulted in an abundance of clothing for the Union soldiers. It also resulted in disgracefully low wages—about 24¢ per day—for women in the garment industry, because there were so many shirts and uniforms being produced.

Women on the home front also held fund-raisers to support the U.S. Sanitary Commission, which was in charge of all

In addition to sewing and doing other traditionally female jobs, women from the South and the North worked in munitions factories. These women are making cartridges for Union muskets at the arsenal in Watertown, Massachusetts.

medical care and supplies for the soldiers. One of the most successful fund drives was the Northwestern Sanitary Commission's fair held in Chicago in 1863. The organizers, Mary Livermore, Jane Hoge, and Eliza Porter, contacted women throughout the Midwest, seeking donations of food and clothing—anything that could be sold. They received bushels of carrots and potatoes, pigs, horses, lace, dresses, jams and jellies, and the first draft of the Emancipation Proclamation from President Lincoln himself. The women had hoped to raise $25,000; the group cleared $100,000, $3,000 just from the sale of Lincoln's donation. The fair's remarkable success inspired others to try similar fund-raisers, and shortly after, fairs were held in many Northern cities to help support the Commission.

Soldiers were not the only people who needed supplies. Fugitive and freed slaves, whose numbers increased dramatically as Union troops pushed southward, needed food, shelter, clothing, and jobs. Various organizations, some run by the federal government, others by private groups, tried to meet the mounting needs. One of these groups, the Contraband Relief Association, was run by Elizabeth Keckley. A former slave, Keckley was a skilled seamstress. After she bought her freedom with money she earned by taking on extra sewing projects, she settled in Richmond. Her customers included Varina Davis. When Elizabeth moved to Washington, one of her clients, who became her good friend, was Mary Todd Lincoln. Noting that many organizations held benefits to raise money, Keckley appealed to local churches to do the same for former slaves. On one occasion, Mary Todd Lincoln allowed her to hold a fundraiser on the White House lawn. Keckley's organization was very successful, and it fed and clothed many former slaves while they tried to find work.

Today many women work for the federal government, but in 1860 the idea of employing women in any office was suspect. Interestingly enough, unlike the textile mills where women were thought to be in need of protection, this time critics feared that men in offices needed safeguarding. Women, the critics argued, would distract and even corrupt male colleagues. After all, what kind of woman would work side by side with men? But the war greatly increased the need for records, and in the absence of copy machines, computers, and even typewriters everything had to done by hand. This work required many people, and because female clerks, like textile workers, would accept low wages, the financially strapped federal government decided to hire women.

In 1861, Francis Spinner, the treasurer of the United States, hired the first female clerks for his department. He eventually employed more than 400 women. Preference was given to widows whose husbands had died in the war. Other departments followed suit, most notably the postal service.

Even though the women proved themselves to be dedicated workers for the government, critics attacked them. In 1864, some believed that there was enough evidence to prove that the Treasury Department was rife with immoral women, who were conducting themselves in the most shocking manner in the office and doing scandalous things in the cloakroom.

Such critics, led by Congressman James Brooks, demanded an investigation. Detectives gathered information by breaking into the apartments of the "government girls" and seizing their diaries and letters. Detectives also wrote confessions and frightened young women into signing them.

At the hearing that followed, the critics were lambasted for their actions and their accusations for which they failed to provide one shred of proof. Brooks's allegations were condemned as "exceedingly unjust and cruel" for they had "compromised the reputation of three hundred females . . . a majority of whom [were] . . . wives or sisters of soldiers fallen in the field."[1] The hearing ended the public attacks on the clerks, but it did not change the critics' opinion of "government girls."

In addition to the clothing, supplies, and clerks it needed, the federal government required large supplies of food to feed its army. To encourage the establishment of more farms, Congress passed the Homestead Act of 1862, which gave 160 acres (65 hectares) of land to anyone who would live on it and farm it. The Act had been delayed in Congress for years by Southern representatives who feared that settlers would rush into Northern territories and create many nonslave states. Between 1862 and the end of the war, more than 15,000 settlers, some of them free blacks, took advantage of the Act, moving primarily to the Midwest. The new farms produced an abundance of food.

The Confederate home front was quite different from that of the Union. The South was dependent on one major crop,

"King Cotton," which to date had been lucrative. As a result, the South saw little need to industrialize on a wide scale, preferring instead to buy the manufactured products that it needed with the huge profits it made from the sale of cotton. But once the war started, the North's naval blockade hampered the Confederacy's ability to buy anything. So from the beginning of the war, the Confederacy struggled to feed, clothe, and arm its soldiers while trying to hold back a determined foe.

Women in the South were eager and willing to help their cause from the home front, and unlike their sisters in the North, their help was actively sought. This was because, in large part, so many men, more than 1 million of the South's 5.5 million white population, were at some time part of the army, causing a severe manpower shortage on the home front.

Southern women made a lot of clothing. At least 4,000 worked as individual contractors, providing fabric or shirts. Some women were employed in Southern textile industries, such as the mill in Saluda, South Carolina. Like many others during the war, all 400 Saluda workers lost their jobs when Union troops invaded and burned the mill. One witness reported seeing "female operatives weeping and wringing their hands in agony as they saw . . . their only means of support in flames."[2]

Southern women also worked in munitions plants, where a number of them lost their lives. An explosion in the Confederate States Laboratory in Richmond, for example, killed forty women, and it was not the only disaster in the South. At the same time, the Union experienced similar tragedies in Pennsylvania and Connecticut, both of which claimed the lives of female workers.

When the need for workers could not be met by women and free blacks, the Confederacy rented slaves. At first, slave owners could decide if they wished to make their slaves available. As the war dragged on and every possible worker was needed, the Confederate government drafted some slaves. These slaves, whose salaries went to their owners, worked in munitions plants, shipyards, mines, and hospitals.

Few blacks, free or slave, were happy about working for the Confederacy. But in some cases, blacks were able to make use of their positions to help the North. One of the most notable of these involved Mary Louveste, a free black who worked in the Gosport Navy Yard where the *Virginia,* an ironclad, was being built. She carefully gathered information about the ship and journeyed to Washington to inform Secretary of the Navy Gideon Welles about the South's latest weapon. Her information helped reduce some of the fear the Union was expected to feel when the *Virginia* was unveiled. After questioning Louveste, Secretary Welles knew that the North's *USS Monitor* could outmaneuver the South's ironclad.

Southern women also were employed by the government. One of the largest employers of female clerks was the Treasury Department. Each paper dollar it printed was signed by hand, and toward the end of the war, the government was printing huge amounts of money, even though much of it was almost worthless since it was backed by little gold.

As the war dragged on and many plantations and businesses lay in ruins, the competition for employment became keen, especially among widows who had families to support. The secretary of the treasury claimed that he had at least 100 applications for each opening in his department. But when the Confederacy collapsed, all government employees lost their jobs.

Although Northern women complained bitterly about rising prices during the war, most had adequate supplies of foodstuffs and clothing to see them through. Southern women, however, saw prices rise and supplies drop dramatically throughout the war. They also lived in constant fear of invasion.

Some could not endure the rigors of the home front, especially near the battle sites. At least 250,000 Southerners, mostly women and children, moved during the war, although

As the war raged on and advanced toward them, thousands of families, most of them in the South and usually led by women, left their homes for safer areas. Those who chose to stay often faced severe shortages of food and other supplies.

deciding where to go was not easy. Dolly Burge, a widow in Georgia, was typical. In her diary, she described her predicament. After witnessing mass troop movements, she wrote: "Saw men going . . . to town. . . . Have been uneasy all day. . . What shall I do? Where go?"[3] Most refugees moved south or west in the Confederacy to avoid the Yankees. Burge moved to Texas. Others left the Confederacy for the Union, settling primarily in Kansas and New York City, where by 1863, about 25,000 Confederates had relocated.

The refugees left behind longtime friends and familiar territory, and they suffered from homesickness. One woman wrote in her diary: "My heart feels often as if it would break with longing for home."[4]

Those who remained in the South had to find ways to cope with the increasing shortages. They made clothes from old sheets and curtains, coloring the fabric with homemade dyes, and turned palmetto leaves into hats to shield themselves from the hot sun. When coffee was no longer available, they made a Confederate variety from roasted particles of corn, peas, or chicory roots.

When all else failed, exhausted, overworked women begged their husbands or sons or brothers to come home to plant crops and feed their families before they all starved. One young woman's plea is typical:

> My dear Edward—I have always been proud of you, and since your connection with the Confederate army, I have been prouder of you than ever before. I would not have you do anything wrong for the world, but . . . last night I was aroused by little Eddie's crying. I called and said, "What is the matter Eddie?" and he said, "O Mamma! I am so hungry." And Lucy, your darling Lucy, she never complains, but she is growing thinner and thinner every day. And before God, Edward, unless you come home, we must die.
>
> Your Mary[5]

The struggle to find enough to eat and be able to pay for it eventually affected even the wealthiest and best known in the South, as Union forces, like those under General William T. Sherman, tried to force the Confederacy to surrender by destroying everything in their path. Mary Chesnut, for example, was forced to exchange some of her clothing for food. General Robert E. Lee's wife, Mary, who was crippled by arthritis, spent most of the war in Richmond, where friends provided financial help. By the end of the war, though, even Mary Lee had serious financial difficulties.

Although Confederate women clearly had their hands full, they still volunteered their time in local hospitals, nursed wounded soldiers in their homes, and devised many ways to raise money to buy war supplies. One of the most popular fund drives was for gunboats, and one Southern woman said that "there was a perfect *furore* throughout the Confederacy for Ladies Gunboat Funds."[6] Such drives were held in most major Southern ports, such as Charleston, Savannah, New Orleans, and Mobile. Other fund-raisers included fairs, bazaars, raffles, and dramatic presentations.

While the women sewed, knit, grew vegetables, and raised money, they worried about loved ones and mourned their losses as did Northern women. And because so many men died, it was unusual for any family to escape tragedy. Incredible as it may seem, records indicate that some women lost as many as five sons during the war.

It's not surprising to learn that Confederate women, eventually seeing no chance to win the war and "sick unto death" of the bloody conflict, wanted peace, even if it meant that they had to surrender. In early 1865, a woman who identified herself only as a "Poor Woman" wrote to the governor of her state, pleading with him to end the war. She said:

> For the sake of suffering humanity . . . and especially for the sake of suffering women and children try and stop this cruel war. Here I am without one mouthful to eat for myself and five children and God only knows where I will get something now. You know . . . that it is impossible to whip the Yankees. . . . My husband has been killed, and if they all [fight] till they are dead what in the name of God will become of us poor women.[7]

"Poor Woman" did not have long to wait. The war was nearly over.

In the spring of 1865, Richmond, the capital city of the Confederacy, was in ruins, as was much of the South. Women who had coped with life during the war, and had seen their country destroyed and their men die in battle, had a difficult time resuming their traditional roles as wives and mothers.

CHAPTER EIGHT

LOSSES AND GAINS

We covered our faces and cried.

Nellie Grey,
Richmond native

The Confederate Army withdrew from Richmond on April 2, 1865. Early the next morning, Union troops entered the capital, which now lay in ruins. Retreating Confederate soldiers had destroyed the munitions that they could not carry to keep them out of the hands of the enemy, and sparks from exploding shells had set buildings on fire. Flames raced through sections of Richmond, destroying everything in their path. The fall of the city was painful for all Southerners, since most believed, correctly, that its capture meant that the surrender of the Confederacy was close at hand.

One of the many women in Richmond who recorded her feelings in her journal was Nellie Grey. Her heartbreak is obvious:

> Exactly at eight o'clock [A.M.] the Confederate flag that fluttered above the Capitol came down and the Stars and Stripes were run up. We knew what that meant! . . . . Richmond was in the hands of the Federals. . . . All through the house was the sound of sobbing. It was as the house of mourning, the house of death. . . .

Was it to this end we had fought and starved and gone naked and cold? to this end that the wives and children of many a dear and gallant friend were husbandless and fatherless? to this end that our homes were in ruins, our State devastated?[1]

An exhausted Robert E. Lee, his country destroyed and his capital in flames, had little choice but to surrender to General Ulysses S. Grant. He did so on April 9. More troops surrendered on April 26, the last on May 26.

While Congress and President Andrew Johnson argued about how best to reunite the country, Northern and Southern women tried to put their lives in order. The public assumed that women would resume their traditional roles as mothers and housewives. But like the Revolutionary War—and the many wars to come—this conflict had brought about new opportunities for women, and many were not willing to give up these gains. Also, because so many men had died, many widows had to work outside the home to support themselves and their families, and thousands of young women would never marry. And there were nearly two million black women whose roles under slavery had been abolished.

Unlike soldiers and spies, for which there was little need now, the demand for nurses and doctors was great. Many wounded men would need care for some time to come. Women who had served on the battlefields—North and South—recognized this need and fought hard for the right to keep working. Although they were accepted initially, they were the first to be laid off as the wounded recovered enough to be sent home.

Female nurses also found work with the Freedmen's Bureau, which had been established in 1865 to help former slaves. As early as 1861, fugitive slaves had begun to arrive at Union forts seeking protection. At one time, more than 900 blacks were being housed at Fort Monroe, near Richmond. Soldiers, with the help of the former slaves, built small villages at the forts or on abandoned plantations in Union-held territory to provide housing. The villages grew dramatically after the war ended, when many blacks sought help. Many former slaves were in poor health when they reached safety, and others, due to crowded living conditions, became ill after they arrived. Nurses were then sent by the bureau to care for the sick.

A handful of army nurses returned to school to become doctors after the war. Most of these sought training in women's schools such as Elizabeth Blackwell's New York Medical College. The number of female students studying to become doctors increased over the years, and by 1900 more than 2,500 women had received medical degrees.

In addition, by 1890, twenty medical schools were accepting female students into their nursing programs. Eventually, this profession would be dominated by women.

Northern women who had jobs in industry fought to keep their gains as well as to improve their working conditions. But the economic slowdown that followed the war, coupled with former soldiers seeking jobs, made it very difficult for women to keep their positions, even if they would work for low wages. Several organizations tried to help them. One of these, the New York Workingwomen's Protective Union, had already begun work during the war, trying to protect female workers from unfair labor practices by seeking help from the courts. It continued to do so after the war.

At the same time, labor unions began to think about letting women join their organizations. Union members were well aware that as long as women would work for less, all wages would be kept low. (For the same reason, Northern workers, men and women alike, did not want blacks to move to industrial centers, fearing that they would work for even less money, causing all wages to plummet.) Although women weren't admitted to unions until 1881, the fact that unions even considered granting them admission was a major victory for female workers.

After the war, Northern investors began to build industries in the South. But Southern women did not rush to the new companies to apply for work. Many had become more conservative than ever after the war, trying to re-create the distant past when life was not so painful. This meant that women stayed home. Others resented working for Northern companies. So by 1870, only about 3,000 Southern women were working in factories. Even twenty years later, there were only 18,000, a sharp contrast to the North, where 300,000 women were employed in industry. At the same time, about 70,000 Southern women were making their living as seamstresses, working primarily in their homes as they had during the war.

Former slaves, the vast majority of whom remained in the South, had no homes in which to work; nor could they readily find jobs in industry since they could not read and write. In fact, there was great confusion about what to do with the former slaves. Cornelia Boaz, who owned a plantation in Virginia, said: "People seem to be at a loss what to do with their servants. We have made no change with ours yet none of them have left excepting Big Jim who has gone to Appomattox to see about his wife & children. . . . It appears to be a general plan to let the servants remain as they are till this fall."[2]

The blacks who remained with former owners helped to plant spring crops. The wages that they earned—or a share of the crop that they could sell—were supposed to provide them with enough money to support themselves. It was a meager living at best. Although most lived in poverty, many would remain on the land that they knew best for many years.

Those who left their former owners had to find work. The Freedmen's Bureau helped by providing them with an education. Schools were established throughout the South for blacks of all ages. Most classrooms were manned by Northern teachers, many of whom were women. The former slaves were eager to learn, and as more showed up in classrooms, more teachers were needed, creating job opportunities for women. Private groups, especially missionary societies, also provided instructors.

Former slaves who had fled to the North needed an education as well. Since public schools would not accept blacks, private schools were established. Some of the teachers, like Fanny Jackson Coppin, were former slaves.

Through the Freedmen's Bureau and other groups, many Northern women traveled to the South to teach former slaves, with the goal of helping them adjust to life as free people. This volunteer from Connecticut is tutoring two women in reading.

At the same time that blacks were seeking work, they were also trying to reunite family members. Although some had managed to keep track of relatives through a remarkably active slave grapevine, most did not know where their relatives were or if they were still alive. In short, it was a time of great turmoil for the former slaves, who had no guidelines to follow while they tried to reunite families and sought to become responsible, productive citizens.

Northern "government girls" had proved their ability during the war, and they expected to remain in their jobs after the war ended. They not only did so, but the number of women hired increased dramatically over the years, doubling by 1875. Other agencies, both state and local, as well as many businesses, followed along and hired female clerks, bookkeepers, stenographers, and receptionists. And because they would work for less money than men, hiring women became a thrifty choice, especially for tax-supported government agencies. Eventually, women would dominate the clerical field. By 1900, about 75 percent of all government office workers were female.

Immediately after the war the federal government hired only a few Southern women, and these had been loyal to the North. Union spy Elizabeth Van Lew, for example, was appointed postmistress of Richmond by President Ulysses S. Grant when he took office. By 1870, though, many Southern women had been hired by the government both to provide them with income and to help bind the country's wounds by treating all women alike, no matter what side they had supported during the conflict.

Southern women had too many immediate problems to cope with to be able to contribute time and money to charitable causes on a large scale after the war. On the other hand, Northern women who had volunteered their services during the war wanted to continue to help others, and many did. Some volunteered to work in the Freedmen's Bureau. Others raised money to help educate the former slaves. And a few raised money to help Southern women. One of these organizations, founded by Mrs. Algernon Sydney Sullivan, called itself the New York Ladies Southern Relief Association. Most of the members were Southern-born women who had moved to the North when they married Northerners. This group raised more than $70,000.

Although the suffragists had put aside their demands to fight for abolition during the war, they resumed their campaign for the right of women to vote as soon as Richmond fell. But their efforts were hampered by at least three factors. First, male abolitionists, after promising to do so, now refused to support the women. Instead of fighting to remove race and sex from voting restrictions, the abolitionists were happy to settle for getting the right to vote for black males. Female suffragists considered this an outright betrayal.

Second, suffragists considered the long list of significant gains that women had made in the previous four years. Afraid that a public backlash would put these at risk if they asked for more, some women refused to push for the vote.

And third, those who remained committed to the cause were deeply divided about how best to accomplish their goal. As a result, the movement was weakened, and the drive for suffrage failed in the postwar era.

While some of the female suffragists marveled at the new opportunities before them, they were well aware of the costs of the war, as were all Americans. Shortly after the war ended, both Southerners and Northerners began the tradition of decorating the graves of those who had died in the conflict as a way of showing respect for the deceased and the cause for which they had died. Called Decoration Day at first, it eventually became the national holiday of Memorial Day. Celebrated on May 30 or the last Monday in May, it honors all the soldiers who gave their lives for their country—including some who donned men's clothing.

Timeline

1860   South Carolina secedes on December 12. Other Southern states begin to vote on secession.

1861   On February 4, delegates from Alabama, Florida, Georgia, Louisiana, Mississippi, and South Carolina meet and agree to form a new nation, the Confederate States of America. In mid-February Mary Todd Lincoln arrives in Washington, DC. On March 2, Texas joins the Confederacy. Fort Sumter, South Carolina, is fired upon on April 12. Shortly after, Virginia, North Carolina, Tennessee, and Arkansas join the Confederacy. In June, Varina Davis becomes First Lady in Richmond, Virginia. Union and Confederate armies include female color bearers in their units. Rose O'Neal Greenhow begins to spy for the Confederacy. Sarah Edmonds, disguised as a male nurse, begins her duties with the Union army. On July 21, the South wins the first battle of the war at Bull Run. Kady Brownell, Marie Tebe, and Loreta Velazquez participate in the battle. Dorothea Dix offers to start female nursing corps for the Union. Clara Barton goes to the front to care for wounded. Dr. Mary Walker offers her services to the Union. Julia Ward Howe writes "The Battle Hymn of the Republic." Sally Tompkins and Phoebe Yates Pember begin their nursing careers with the Confederate army.

1862   The Union starts its drive to take control of the upper South and the Mississippi River. Mary Bickerdyke begins her work for the Union army in Illinois. Belle Boyd begins to spy for the Confederacy, while Elizabeth

Van Lew gathers information for the Union. On March 11, Union troops prepare to march on Richmond, Virginia, the Confederate capital. They encounter strong resistance outside Richmond on June 26, and on July 7, they retreat, ending the first of many attempts to take the city. Union forces also encounter fierce fighting in the upper South, but manage to declare victory at Shiloh, Tennessee, on April 7. On April 26, Union naval forces capture New Orleans. In late August, Jennie Hodgers enlists in an Illinois regiment. Marie Ravenal de la Coste writes the song "Somebody's Darling," which becomes a big hit in the North and the South.

1863   Suffragists meet in New York to form Women's National Loyal League. Mary Abigail Dodge pleads with Union Women to support the war in an essay, "A Call to My Country-women." On July 3, a major Confederate attack on the North is turned back at Gettysburg, Pennsylvania. On July 4, Union forces under General Ulysses S. Grant take Vicksburg, Mississippi, the last Confederate stronghold on the Mississippi River, after a six-week siege. The battles at Gettysburg and Vicksburg are turning points in the war. The Confederacy is seriously weakened. Belle Boyd and Rose O'Neal Greenhow write books about their espionage activities. Volunteers hold a fair in Chicago to raise money for the Union's Sanitary Commission.

1864   Investigation of Union's "government girls" begins. On May 5, General Grant starts another Union drive toward Richmond. At the battle at Cold Harbor, Virginia, June 1-3, Grant loses 12,000 men in one day. Because his losses are so high, Grant now decides to lay siege to Richmond rather than use armed forces to take it. From May 7 until December 22, Union general William T. Sherman marches from Tennessee to Atlanta and Savannah, Georgia. He destroys everything of any value to the Confederates along the way.

1865   From January 16 until March 21, Sherman marches northward through the Carolinas, again destroying anything that might help the Confederates. Southern woman identified only as "Poor Woman" asks Confederate government to surrender. On April 2, the Confederates abandon Richmond. Nellie Grey witnesses the fall of the Confederate capital. On April 9, Robert E. Lee surrenders his troops to Grant at Appomattox, Virginia. The rest of the Confederate soldiers surrender to Sherman on April 26. On April 14, President Lincoln is shot. On May 10, Jefferson Davis is captured in Georgia. On May 26, the last Confederate troops surrender.

Notes

CHAPTER ONE

1. Elizabeth Van Lew, Papers, New York Public Library.
2. Catherine Clinton, *The Other Civil War: American Women in the Nineteenth Century* (New York: Hill and Wang, 1984), p. 147.
3. Harriet Sigerman, *An Unfinished Battle: American Women 1848–1865* (New York: Oxford University Press, 1994), p. 20.

CHAPTER TWO

1. C. Vann Woodward, editor, *Mary Chesnut's Civil War* (New Haven, CT: Yale University Press, 1981), p. 99.
2. Richard Hall, *Patriots in Disguise* (New York: Marlowe & Company, 1994), p. 109.
3. Hall, pp. 108, 109.
4. Mary Elizabeth Massey, *Bonnet Brigades: American Women and the Civil War* (New York: Alfred A. Knopf, 1966), p. 30.
5. Massey, p. 39.
6. Robert P. Broadwater, *Daughters of the Cause: Women in the Civil War* (Martinsburg, PA: Daisy Publishing, 1993), p. 16.
7. Hall, p. 104.
8. Patricia W. Romero and Willie Lee Rose, *A Black Woman's Civil War Memoirs: Susie King Taylor* (Princeton, NJ: Markus Wiener Publishers, Inc., 1988), p. 61.

CHAPTER THREE

1. Richard Hall, *Patriots in Disguise* (New York: Marlowe & Company, 1994), pp. 67, 68.
2. Katharine M. Jones, *Ladies of Richmond* (Indianapolis: Bobbs–Merrill Company, Inc., 1962), pp. 117, 118.

CHAPTER FOUR

1. Elizabeth D. Leonard, *Yankee Women: Gender Battles in the Civil War* (New York: W. W. Norton & Company, 1994), p. 15.
2. Robert P. Broadwater, *Daughters of the Cause: Women in the Civil War* (Martinsburg, PA: Daisy Publishing, 1993), p. 3.

3. John R. Brumgardt, editor, *Civil War Nurse: The Diary and Letters of Hannah Ropes* (Knoxville: University of Tennessee Press, 1980), p. 40.

4. Broadwater, p. 4.

5. Mary Elizabeth Massey, *Bonnet Brigades: American Women and the Civil War* (New York: Alfred A. Knopf, 1966), p. 49.

6. Leonard, pp. 129, 130.

7. Leonard, pp. 138, 139.

8. James West Davidson and Mark H. Lytle, *The United States: A History of the Republic* (Englewood Cliffs, NJ: Prentice–Hall, Inc., 1981), p. 336.

CHAPTER FIVE

1. C. Vann Woodward, editor, *Mary Chesnut's Civil War* (New Haven, CT: Yale University Press, 1981), p. 13.

2. Justin G. Turner and Linda Levitt Turner, editors, *Mary Todd Lincoln: Her Life and Letters* (New York: Alfred A. Knopf, 1972), p. 122.

3. Bell Irwin Wiley, *Confederate Women* (Westport, CT: Greenwood Press, 1975), pp. 83, 84.

4. Wiley, pp. 102, 103.

5. Ruth Painter Randall, *I Varina: A Biography of the Girl Who Married Jefferson Davis and Became the First Lady of the South* (Boston: Little, Brown and Company, 1962), p. 203.

CHAPTER SIX

1. Elliott Ashkenazi, editor, *The Civil War Diary of Clara Solomon: Growing Up in New Orleans 1861–1862* (Baton Rouge: Louisiana State University Press, 1995), p. 17.

2. Ashkenazi, p. 370.

3. Irwin Silber, compiler and editor, *Songs of the Civil War* (New York: Columbia University Press, 1960), p. 146.

4. Madelon Golden Schilpp and Sharon M. Murphy, *Great Women of the Press* (Carbondale: Southern Illinois University, 1983), p. 82.

5. C. Vann Woodward, editor, *Mary Chesnut's Civil War* (New Haven, CT: Yale University Press, 1981), pp. 514, 515, 517.

CHAPTER SEVEN

1. Mary Elizabeth Massey, *Bonnet Brigades: American Women and the Civil War* (New York: Alfred A. Knopf, 1966), p. 138.

2. Massey, p. 149.

3. Katharine M. Jones, *When Sherman Came: Southern Women and the "Great March"* (Indianapolis: The Bobbs-Merrill Company, Inc., 1964), p. 9.

4. Bell Irwin Wiley, *Confederate Women* (Westport, CT: Greenwood Press, 1975), pp. 151, 152.

5. Wiley, p. 177.

6. Massey, p. 37.

7. Wiley, p. 176.

CHAPTER EIGHT

1. Katharine M. Jones, *Ladies of Richmond* (Indianapolis: Bobbs Merrill Company, Inc., 1962), pp. 281, 282.

2. Ervin L. Jordan, Jr., *Black Confederates and Afro-Yankees in Civil War Virginia* (Charlottesville: University Press of Virginia), p. 300.

FURTHER READING

For more information about some of the women mentioned in this book, check out the following biographies: *Harriet Tubman* by Burns Bree (New York: Chelsea Juniors, 1992); *Mary Todd Lincoln, Girl of the Bluegrass* by Katharine E. Wilkie (New York: Aladdin Books, 1992); *Spy for the Confederacy: Rose O'Neal Greenhow* by Jeanette C. Nolan (New York: Julian Messner, 1960); *Clara Barton* by Rafael Tilton (San Diego: Lucent, 1995); *Behind Rebel Lines: The Incredible Story of Emma Edmonds, Civil War Spy* by Seymour Reit (New York: Harcourt Brace Jovanovich, 1988); and *Elizabeth Van Lew: Southern Belle, Union Spy* by Karen Zeinert (Parsippany, NJ: Dillon Press, 1995).

To learn more about the war, read Edward Dolan's book, *The American Civil War* (Brookfield, CT: Millbrook, 1997). Also see *The Day Fort Sumter Was Fired On: A Photo History of the Civil War* by James Haskins (New York: Scholastic, 1995). This book examines the main events of the war and discusses its effects on blacks, women, and children.

More than 150 songs were written about the Civil War during the conflict, a number of which were composed by women. They reflect the women's love for their country, fears for their loved ones, and their hope for peace. To hear some of these songs, listen to *Civil War Music: Collector's Edition*, a CD published by Time–Life Music (1987).

INDEX